Quiet Street

Quiet Street

ON AMERICAN PRIVILEGE

Nick McDonell

Pantheon Books   *New York*

Library of Congress Cataloging-in-Publication Data
Name: McDonell, Nick, [date] author.
Title: Quiet street : on American privilege / Nick McDonell.
Description: New York : Pantheon Books, 2023
Identifiers: LCCN 2022053277 (print). LCCN 2022053278 (ebook).
ISBN 9780593316788 (hardcover). ISBN 9780593316795 (ebook).
Subjects: LCSH: Elite (Social sciences)—New York (State)—New York. |
Power (Social sciences)—New York (State)—New York. | Rich people—
New York (State)—New York—History. | Social classes—
New York (State)—New York—History.
Classification: LCC HN90.E4 M336 2023 (print) |
LCC HN90.E4 (ebook) | DDC 305.5/2097471—dc23/eng/20230127
LC record available at https://lccn.loc.gov/2022053277
LC ebook record available at https://lccn.loc.gov/2022053278

www.pantheonbooks.com

Jacket image: Five/Moment/Getty Images
Jacket design by Janet Hansen

Printed in the United States of America
First Edition
2 4 6 8 9 7 5 3 1

Or perhaps a person can write about things only when she is no longer the person who experienced them, and that transition is not yet complete. The person who writes about her experience is not the same person who had the experience. The ability to write about it is proof of change, of great distance. Not everyone is willing to admit this, but it's true.

In this sense, a conversion narrative is built into every autobiography: the writer purports to be the one who remembers, who saw, who did, who felt, but the writer is no longer that person. In writing things down, she is reborn. And yet still defined by the actions she took, even if she now distances herself.

—Rachel Kushner, *The Hard Crowd: Essays 2000–2020*

PREFACE

In the first spring of the pandemic, I worked a few shifts at a hospital in Brooklyn. The governor had asked on television that health care workers volunteer, and tens of thousands did. I was surely among the least qualified—an EMT on paper, I had till then worked a total of twelve hours, a single overnight ambulance rotation amid the bars and projects of Manhattan's Lower East Side. Over the course of that night we transported ten or so patients to various hospitals. I bandaged the forearm and hand of a stabbing victim; lifted and wheeled a diabetic drunk; commiserated with a repeat psychiatric patient who said the government was spying on him, which, in one form or another, it probably was. This was the limit of my clinical experience. And so when an official from the New York Medical Reserve Corps called with my assignment, based on the form I'd submitted online, my first thought was: If they're calling *me,* the situation must be a little bit dire. At the hospital, the human resources official with whom I checked in thanked me and then, somewhat sheepishly, asked if I was willing to work in the morgue. That's where they could really use the help, she explained. I had been looking forward to treating the living but on quick reflection supposed the dead were more commensurate with my level of experience and agreed to go wherever she thought best.

The work itself left little time for reflection. It consisted of bagging, moving, tagging, and inventorying corpses. The main problem, for me, was goggles. Mine fogged up. We were advised, however, not to touch our goggles once we had them on, lest we bring the virus from our hands to our faces. And so, as the first shift progressed, rather than adjust my goggles, I tilted my chin ever higher into the air, peering down my nose through a shrinking, unfogged window. I envied one of my colleagues his superior ski goggles. Through the fog, it was almost impossible to see what I was doing. The morgue itself was well lit, but the hallways were dim and the refrigerated trailer into which we loaded the bodies was dark. We wore headlamps but tripped consistently over the plywood ramp we'd fashioned to get the gurneys inside the trailer. In order to identify names Sharpied onto tags and bags, I had to bring my face right up close, which, of course, was the last thing I wanted to do. My mask obscured, mostly, the distinctive smell of death—but not entirely. Compromised of sight and smell, I lumbered about in my hazmat suit, unable to hear my colleagues' directions, which, muffled by masks, had to be repeated at increasing volume. There were so many bodies that we had to lay some on the floor, presenting ourselves with an additional tripping hazard.

My partner on the first shift was Michael (whose name, like some others in this book, I've changed for the sake of privacy). When our supervisor introduced us in the hallway outside her tiny basement office, he was shadowboxing. This did not inspire a great deal of confidence, but Michael was both competent and, from what I could tell, well liked. On the two occasions we transported patients rather than corpses, he charmed them in spite of their severe illness and discomfort. He was Black, Jamaican, joked and teased constantly. He was a master fish fryer, he said, and had made a smart real estate investment in Atlanta, which he showed me via live security cam feed on his phone. He wanted to know about my romantic life and if I had "shot up the club," which, he clarified, meant gotten my girlfriend pregnant. In the breakroom he announced the equality of all people and mocked the president, who appeared sometimes on the wall-mounted TV between sitcom reruns. Michael also pointed out the flyer, pinned to the bulletin board, that memorialized his friend and colleague who had that month died of the coronavirus. Next to this flyer was another, apparently authored by a union, arguing that health workers like Michael should be receiving hazard pay during the pandemic. They weren't. Michael spoke in a baritone and sometimes liked to sing while we waited or worked, in the style of '70s protest songs. "Corona, Corona / Be killin' the people!" He told me he had been at the hospital seventeen years and in that time raised a son who was now doing similar work at another hospital.

He also made sure I had one of the good masks. These were in short supply and kept in a box under the desk of a regal salt-and-pepper-haired lady named Stella who administered the ER. She teased me when I arrived, along the lines of a lascivious "*mm-hmm, he can work for me,*" even suggesting that when I next came, I should bring champagne and rope, as though one of us might tie the other up for pleasure. I regretted immediately saying that I would bring the rope. Stella called most people who passed her desk in the center of the ER "baby." Michael referred to colleagues the same way and told me more than once the hospital was a big family. My other colleagues in the morgue, all seconded there to deal with the flood of the dead, were less sentimental. I sensed, in fact, that even if they liked Michael, they found him a little annoying—a bit like an overly opinionated uncle at a holiday dinner. I noted too that Michael preferred, understandably, not to move bodies into the trailer and sometimes, when possible, left this onerous task to younger men.

First among them was the owner of the ski goggles—Jawann. He was our leader, coordinating our efforts, counting off the lifts. "One, two, three," Jawann would say, and we'd hoist a body. He was on the verge of finishing his nursing degree and, perhaps of necessity, better organized than the rest of us. Everyone liked him, but I cannot have been the only one who envied his goggles. By the second half of each shift, I gave up trying to see through my own and moved them up onto my forehead. The rest of my colleagues fared little better, eye-protection-wise—their flimsy plastic face shields, provided by the hospital, tended to skew and fall off. Bare-eyed, we felt an especial urgency to finish, for the longer we spent among the dead, the more likely, it seemed to us, we would contract the virus that had killed all these people. I confess that, in our hurry, we may have once misplaced a body, or rather, mislabeled one. But by the time we realized the paperwork didn't make sense, that the count might be off, we had been in the trailer a long time. One of the bags had ripped; evil-looking fluids dripped and pooled on the floor. A look passed between us. Probably it was fine. Time to get out of the trailer.

I will leave out of this introductory sketch the time one of the trailer shelves broke, dropping one body onto another, as well as the maddening process of removing a hazmat suit, the pedestrians who gawped at our work through the chain-link fence, the Eastern European–accented undertaker who palmed me a twenty for the speed with which we produced the corpses he had come to collect in his cardboard coffins, Michael's disquisition on Bob Marley's genius, Jawann's advice on the mental preparation required to deal with the dead, the husband and wife we tried to keep together in the sea of body bags, and all the awful rest of it. When I volunteered, I thought I might collect such incidents and turn them into a book about life in that hospital, a kind of practitioner's memoir. But by my fourth shift, it seemed to me that, to do so properly, I would have to work there for years—to become, however much I could, a member of the community, which was majority Black and Latinx and not wealthy—and I was not prepared to do so. Moreover, I wondered whether, even if I *did* stay for years, I could write about this community well or usefully, being as I was of a different race and economic class, an outsider.

I was, in a sense, a professional outsider. For over a decade I'd reported and written about Iraqis and Afghans caught in the American wars. But recently I'd stopped, no longer thinking myself an appropriate person to tell their stories. I had for a long time been grappling with the idea that as a white man of financial privilege—more on this term to come—it would be better—more on that to come too—for me to do some kind of intrinsically useful work, like EMT-ing, and leave cultural work, like writing, to people who suffered injustice; or at least, combine the two. For, rather than experience injustice, I had in many ways been its beneficiary. As a volunteer in the hospital, I didn't dwell on this fact. As a writer, however, matters were more complicated. Even if I was volunteering in the morgue, I was also there, partly, to write. Was I then a tourist—or worse, a kind of profiteer?

As the pandemic ebbed in New York, a summer of protests began. The protestors demanded that America reckon with its history of racial and economic injustice, and I marched too, sometimes. I wondered, though, if I had reckoned sufficiently with myself—or, perhaps more important, with the community that had produced me, which was so very far removed from that hospital and those protests. It seemed a good time to take a look at where I'd come from; to do some excavation at my own two feet. And so I decided to stop the hospital work, for a while at least, and just write. But rather than write about injustice as experienced by those people who bore its brunt, I would attend to my own people. I would write about the one percent, among whom I had been raised.

What, exactly, is the one percent? I was surprised, the first time I looked at the numbers. As of 2022, the income threshold, globally, was about $170,000 per year, per adult. For the United States, it was higher, about $500,000. But income is only one part of wealth. The World Inequality Lab, based out of the Paris School of Economics and the University of California, Berkeley, had set up a useful online tool: "Where are you in the income and wealth distribution? Use our comparator to position yourself relative to others."

I entered my data. I was born in 1984 in New York City and earned money by writing screenplays, magazine articles, and books—like this one, for which I am being paid $175,000 over three years. In 2013, I bought a house for $910,000, and had about $300,000 in an IRA account, and about $150,000 in stocks—all purchased with money I'd made from novels written in my teens and early twenties. My parents had paid for my education and loaned me half the down payment on the house. According to the distribution tool, I was in the 96th percentile of wealth in the United States, and the 99th worldwide.

In the context I'm about to describe, I wasn't—had never been—particularly wealthy. The American one percent was itself highly unequal, its wealth concentrated among the roughly sixteen thousand families making up the .01 percent—and even more so among the billionaires, two of whom I knew before I understood, in my gut rather than my head, just how unusual all this was.

Some people I care for will likely recognize themselves in these pages. If they feel betrayed, I hope they agree that interrogation of our class is necessary to a more just society, and is to be desired. They say they are for justice; I take them at their word. The question I put to them is what it means to be of the one percent—what is owed the other ninety-nine, and ourselves?

I

The opulence of New York City is famous. Countless streaming programs, articles, novels, films, and social media feeds are dedicated to the markers of American oligarchy. Shows and films like *Succession, The Devil Wears Prada, The Wolf of Wall Street;* TikTok videos like *what your rich mom coffee shop says about you:* "If you get your coffee at Via, you're a seventeen-year-old who is probably richer than me"; novels like *The Bonfire of the Vanities* and *Breakfast at Tiffany's.* Some examples of the genre, like *The Great Gatsby,* are staples of public education. The wealth is not a secret; neither is the inevitable violent decadence. I remember a schoolmate who bragged about defecating in bed so the maid would have to clean it up. Such behavior extended to the highest reaches of power, as was clear in President Trump's casual sexism and violence. One of his children and one of his grandchildren attended the same school as I and the aforementioned defecator.

Still, I have affection for this school, which was called Buckley. It had a reputation for rigor, conservatism, old wealth, and athletic dominance over the dozen or so "top tier" private schools in the city. All sat in a highly developed hierarchy. "Chapin girls marry doctors, Brearley girls become doctors, Spence girls have affairs with doctors," went one well-known saying about those particular girls' schools. Still, all the schools had more in common than not, and if a child attended any one of them, he'd be well prepared to achieve, maintain, and perhaps surpass his parents' position in society. This preparation was accomplished as much by what was *not* taught as what was.

For example. At Buckley, we had Quiet Street. It began with a turn we'd make on the charter buses—not yellow school buses—that we rode out to our playing fields most weekdays of the fall and spring. A right turn onto 124th Street in East Harlem. As we turned, one of the coaches—"sport-sirs," we called them—would announce "quiet street," and that bus, full of white adolescent boys, fell silent. No whacking of shoulder pads or lacrosse sticks, no trash talk, no jokes, no whispers, no pantomimes. Long before, some boy had called a racial epithet out the window, and a Black pedestrian, in response, had thrown something at the bus.

Or so I heard, long after I graduated. As a student, I never learned the details of the story. It was not widely or formally discussed. No one ever explained, and few asked. I knew only that to speak on Quiet Street was forbidden. In ten years at the school, on nearly a thousand bus trips, I remember none of my peers breaking the rule. Such was its mysterious power.

What was going on? I recently asked some of my old classmates. All remembered Quiet Street, and some vague version of the origin story above. One said this:

> Seems kind of silly, and also, I don't know, vaguely racist, maybe? You're basically like, "If we're not quiet on this street then the horrible people who live here are going to jump us," you know what I mean? . . . Maybe not even vaguely racist. Maybe overtly?

My classmate understates the problem. Quiet Street was the manifestation of a culture that preferred silence to discussion of race and class. These issues could not be discussed without raising questions that might undermine, even reveal as hollow, the school's motto: *Honor et Veritas,* or "Honor and Truth." But the nation's inequalities and injustices were so vast, obvious, and incendiary that they could not, credibly, be ignored. And so Quiet Street both acknowledged and elided the violence of society, through memorial silence.

I recently received a school-community-wide email from Buckley's headmaster, emphasizing the importance of diversity and explaining steps taken in response to the murder of George Floyd. In my own eighth-grade class, thirty students were white and three were people of color—of Chinese, Filipino, and Guyanese descent, respectively. Today, according to the school, 34 percent of families self-report a non-white parent. Other things have changed too. The Lord's Prayer rotates with those of other religions at Friday assembly. The school closes for Jewish holidays. As of 2001, female faculty have been permitted to wear pants, rather than dresses or skirts, to work. And though no one is quite sure when it ended, Quiet Street, I am told, no longer exists.

Officially, it never did. There were a lot of powerful, off-the-books rules like that, so powerful they didn't even seem like rules. They seemed almost like physical laws, like gravity—norms, a social scientist might call them—and they governed our lives long after we left Quiet Street and on-ramped to the Triborough Bridge. Thereafter, we filled the bus again with noise and crossed the Harlem River to Randalls Island, to our playing fields. These happened to look out on another island: Rikers—a prison complex, where, of some six thousand inmates, 90 percent are Black or Latinx.

In *The Politics,* Aristotle observed that citizens "who enjoy too many advantages—strength, wealth, connexions, and so forth—are both unwilling to obey, and ignorant how to obey, the law." Children at schools like Buckley, however, had few problems with "the law," and almost never ended up anywhere like Rikers Island. They could, for fun, kick garbage cans into traffic on Park Avenue in the velvet dusk of a spring weekday and suffer no consequences. They could be arrested for, say, vandalism and underage intoxication, mouth off to the arresting officer—"Yeah, I got a bazooka in my pocket"—and be released without charge from the local precinct into the care of a teenage sibling. Passing into adolescence, such children often developed a sense of invincibility. This is common enough among adolescents but lasted, in some of the people I grew up with, deep into adulthood. The shock, rage, and chagrin expressed by the rare one percenter sent to prison were genuine. They were *genuinely surprised* that the world did not bend to their will, as it had since childhood. One schoolmate of mine, convicted of murder despite his insanity plea, famously wrote a letter to the Manhattan district attorney noting that he too was "a graduate of Buckley"—as though this were a basis on which to begin clearing up the charge. The connection usually didn't have to be mentioned, and especially not in writing. On the off chance no mutual friend existed to make a necessary introduction, there were other ways to signal membership in the tribe.

These were drilled for years—the handshake, for example. Teachers manned the door each morning and might deny a student entry until he had shaken hands and voiced a greeting to the teacher's satisfaction.

"Good morning, sir." Firm grip, direct eye contact, tie knotted, ten years old.

"Good morning, Mr. McDonell."

The best manners teach empathy. We learned some,

and mostly grew up into kind men. This did not mean we grew up into *good* men. But kindness, interpersonally, was easy because, generally, everyone was kind to *us*. While all families are worlds unto themselves, we were universally spared the societal traumas of racism, poverty, state violence. We never even had to wait in line, really. We were handled with silk gloves at the Knickerbocker Cotillion dance classes. We ate the freshest vegetables and seafood. Our world was gentle, and so, while there was some bullying, we were usually gentle with each other.

We were also taught to help anyone we saw in distress. This was one of several reasons *whom* we saw was so carefully circumscribed. Really we were blinkered, even as our chivalrous good manners were explicitly connected to the Gospel of Luke—"to whom much is given, much is expected," as quoted by Christopher Wray, director of the FBI, a Buckley boy, at a recent graduation. We were expected to excel, to give back, to serve.

But to serve whom? The only people we knew, outside The Bubble, were the people who served us. We were not boarding with the rest of the passengers. And consider that, failing the handshake test, a student *was not allowed into the building*. He was sent around the block, perhaps in the snow—as I was, January 1996, penny loafers soaked. What, then, was a child to make of someone who didn't know—who was never taught—the proper way to shake hands? Should they be let in, out of the snow?

There is a violence to good manners. A thank-you note, standing up when a woman enters the room, holding the door—we learned soon enough that these thoughtful practices could also be pieces of armor, or tools that might allow you, say, to get your younger brother out of the precinct without a problem. It was not, of course, using the word *sir* that did it. It was what loomed behind a white sixteen-year-old in an Armani tie—power. In certain contexts, a properly executed handshake sent a message not unlike a snake's rattle.

The handshake was the most basic tool. I heard parents put it this way: "I wanted to raise them so that they knew how to do everything." And by college, it must be said, the level of competence was sometimes very high. Twenty-year-olds who could, variously, sail long distances, play the piano, read Latin and Greek, speak French, Mandarin, et cetera. They could play all the games: tennis, football, racquets, court tennis, chess, backgammon, bridge. They could confidently deliver a eulogy, a toast, a speech on nearly any matter of the day, and were excellent drivers, even, very occasionally, pilots. They knew how to read architectural drawings—from the renovations—and were familiar with pistols, rifles, shotguns, dog training, falconry, cigars, esoteric precious stones, horses and horsemanship, wines, cocktails, cinema, first aid, where and in what style to have suits and shoes made and repaired, basic psychopharmacology, how to cook and serve dinner for twenty, by oneself, or with "help," discreet polyamory, tax strategy for the estate and individual, the real estate market and how to access it in several cities, both American and European, art history, alpine and cross-country skiing, how to ask a favor from a chief of staff, flower arranging, attractive use of social media. And on and on. World-class pimple popping, masturbation, and video-gaming too.

Such skills arose not from any extraordinary talent or discipline but from the enormous resources invested in each child. And though I have here emphasized traditionally highbrow skills, we were groomed to be comfortable at every level of culture, in every room—to appreciate Taylor Swift as well as Tchaikovsky, to make small talk with the custodian as well as the senator. The deeper lessons were confidence, poise in any context, what sociologist Shamus Rahman Khan calls *ease*. Old-fashioned exclusionary markers could in fact be a liability, in the same way an all-white classroom was. All the world was ours *not* because of what we excluded or inherited but because of our open-minded good manners and how hard we worked—which, all agreed, was very hard indeed. This superficial meritocracy masked, especially to ourselves, a profound entitlement.

Per class, one or two students came by way of scholarship—usually people of color and, unlike the rest of us, familiar with life beyond The Bubble. Though classes were very small, and friendships ostensibly close, paying students generally had no idea what the home lives of scholarship students were like. Why go all the way to Queens to play *GoldenEye*—the James Bond video game—on Friday afternoon, instead of four blocks north up Park Avenue? A child's imagination is both powerful and unfocused, open to direction. I never imagined what it was like to commute from Queens to school, even though one of our classmates, my friend, was doing exactly this, five days a week. I remember sensing some tenderness, maybe some combination of pride and defensiveness, in how he said his father (I'm paraphrasing) *took care of banks, like the actual buildings*. Or perhaps I only imagined it was defensiveness; after all, I'd never talked to a peer who was connected at all to any kind of blue-collar work. Most everyone else's dad was in finance—though not mine. This was important to me, but I didn't, back then, know why. Once, being driven to a country house near Tuxedo Park, I said to the other kids in the backseat that journalists, like my father, walked into their offices with less pride than investment bankers. I can't recall how I phrased it, exactly, but I imitated the characters—the journalists, the bankers—respectively hanging my head or jutting my jaw.

My father the journalist, however, did *not* hang his head. He was proud. And overhearing, the father at the wheel, a hedge fund manager, interjected into our child's conversation, "Those guys don't have any complexes."

I went silent, embarrassed to be shot down in front

of my peers. Interpreting the exchange now, I suppose he meant simply that journalists were proud of their profession. For my part, I think I was trying to ingratiate myself with both the financier and the scholarship student sitting next to me, by flattering the former and pretending to "lower status" with the latter. This was complicated but typical. We were intensely aware that a hierarchy existed, talked about it—but never about the scholarship family's place in it. We acknowledged our own positions, our power, that is, our *privilege,* only as it suited us. We certainly didn't consider its consequences for the scholarship kids, or why they might have felt uncomfortable eating lunch in the auditorium, served by jacketed kitchen and maintenance staff—all, save one, people of color—whom we called, for what proximate reason I can't remember, "the wombats."

The auditorium was an important place, and not just because of lunch. It was where we staged plays, debated, and, perhaps most important, held our award ceremonies. The school awarded gold, silver, and bronze pins for general scholarship, and prizes for excellence in Latin, composition, public speaking, and so on. But the most highly coveted awards, which got your name engraved on a cup in a glass case, or a plaque on a wall, were for "character." All were named after a boy, teacher, or family who had come before: *The Thomas P. Tammen Cup, given to the boys who have shown outstanding character, achievement, talent, and promise.* These highest awards all traded in words like that—courage, kindness, fairness, generosity—and some of us took them very seriously.

But these values, from nearly the very beginning, caused a dissonance, clashing as they did with our experience. Because once you walked to school—rather than got dropped off, like me, by the black car your father took to midtown—it was possible, likely, that at some point you would see a homeless person, few though there were in the neighborhood. It was impossible not to see poverty along the streets, or race and class among our classmates—some of whom flew on jets to Jackson Hole, while others only ever rode the subway. Such inequality did not feel consistent with prizes for fairness or generosity. The dissonance could become quite powerful. Reflexively repeated gratitude didn't drown it out.

There were essentially three strategies for dealing with it. The first—*insulation*—was to avoid any experience that might puncture The Bubble and so complicate the values we were taught. This was accomplished, mostly, by physical separation, even in densely populated New York. For example—one evening each autumn, Buckley rented Central Park's Wollman Rink, so that we children, skating grinning circles through the bright, merry cold, had that iconic venue entirely to ourselves. It seemed like there was a private entrance, or exclusive time, wherever we went. The consistency of the separation was a marvel, testament to the attention and resources of its keepers, for city life was boisterous and came right to the edges of our own lives, though we did not know it at the time.

Still, there was but one world; total insulation was impossible. Which brings us to the second strategy for dealing with the dissonance—*justification*—wherein the concentration of wealth around us was presented as good and/or necessary. Following this second strategy, it was *not* dissonant to teach kids to worship "fair play" at a school that cost tens of thousands of dollars annually—more than $55,000 in 2022–2023—a few miles from the poorest congressional district in the United States. It was, instead, wise—of a piece with the rising tide that lifted all boats, or trickle-down economics, or "the best of bad options." The theories, more or less well articulated by our elders, were renamed and repackaged over time but shared DNA with their earlier, uglier incarnations, e.g., "the white man's burden" or "separate but equal." At first, we internalized these ideas without knowing their names. In the ninth grade, for example, on a trip to Washington, D.C., it was arranged that my class should meet with Strom Thurmond, one of the country's longest-serving Republican senators. The Senate was impressive but some of us had already inherited the attitude of those parents who said that being a politician was dirty, thankless work. I remember this exchange, recounted years later by a British alumnus of a similar private school:

"Daddy, what do you think, should I be a member of Parliament?"

"Why would you get down in the muck, darling?"

Thurmond was in a wheelchair and an aide pushed him out to meet us. He was most famous, perhaps, for launching history's longest filibuster, in opposition to the 1957 Civil Rights Act, and in defense of segregation. We listened to him attentively, forgot what he said, stayed in a luxury/business hotel, rode the train back to New York, and did not discuss segregation. The lesson was: This is normal. Any one of us could become a senator, power was our birthright. And so it appeared to be. Buckley educated shipping tycoons, newspaper publishers, bank presidents, university deans, Roosevelts, Rockefellers, Trumps. So did the other elite private schools. The Obamas sent their daughters to a somewhat similar, equally expensive school in Washington, D.C.

They, however, and a minority of others, pursued strategy three, which was not justification but *reform* of entrenched power structures—to a degree, anyway. This never had any effect that we could see. As children, we teased each other about being Republicans or Democrats, ignorant of any other groups, but knew that, for us, the distinction was unimportant. The words were meaningless; our lives would never change—even if, executing strategy three, some adults were involved in philanthropic and civic projects, and vocal about passing on a tradition of service to the next generation. At most schools there was a public service requirement alongside the typical coursework. But as Anand Giridharadas detailed in his book *Winners Take All,* the reality of this service was often self-enrichment: "All around us, the winners in our highly inequitable status quo declare themselves partisans of change. . . . Because they are in charge of these attempts at social change, the attempts naturally reflect their biases."

As a consequence of these strategies—especially the first, *insulation*—substantive relationships with people outside the one percent were quite rare. Nannies and teachers were the exception, and it was notable that some of them, at least some of the time, could not help but cast light on the whole shimmering Bubble, even as they kept it afloat.

One such teacher was Mr. Sidoli. He seemed to oscillate between strategies one, two, and three; perhaps the internal tension accounted for his dramatically shifting moods, which ranged from blackest despair to manic enthusiasm for algebra, trigonometry, and basic geometry. He threw chalk with a whizzing, magnificent precision in which, we could tell, he took some pride. If you were staring dreamily out the window he might, mid-word in an explanation of the quadratic equation, sidearm a piece at you with such force as to break it in the center of your forehead. The erasers, when they connected, sent up satisfying clouds of dust.

Once he threw a dictionary but seemed immediately to regret the impulsive act of disrespect for a book. He was white, like all but two of our teachers, and middle-aged, married, with two young boys. We speculated that his marriage was in trouble because we saw him, at least once, sleeping in his car, in the chalk-stained pin-striped suit he often wore. He was wiry, balding, powerfully jawed, and—it was clear from his throwing arm—fairly athletic. Unlike most of the teachers, he was frequently ill-shaven and sported great bags beneath his eyes, which he often widened in feigned shock or rage precipitated by our boyish transgressions.

These were minor enough. We often sensed that Sidoli *himself* was transgressing the norms of the school more gravely. Less by the chalk throwing—we were acculturated to physical violence through our athletic department—than by what he told us. Student opinion was strongly divided over whether he was "full of shit" or not, but everyone was rapt during his digressions from coursework. These were legend, beginning with the antics of his insatiable, giant-testicled goats, which he kept on a farm upstate. Also the mystery and grandeur of the Fibonacci sequence; the history of jazz; the perils of cannabis—a joint of which he confiscated and, we suspected, smoked, though he only ever smelled of cigarettes. He did not report the offending boy, ensuring our collective gratitude. There was a zero-tolerance policy for drugs, except, of course, there wasn't. One day he spent the class warning us that pornography would distort our expectations of and relationships with women—one of the few times I remember a faculty member bringing up the opposite sex. Sidoli is now dead. Shortly before he passed away, an upstate newspaper reported that he was arrested for running a twenty-three-plant cannabis farm in Delaware County, New York. For some of us he was an oddity, for others a provocateur of lasting influence.

Sidoli taught at Buckley for twelve years, and this was not uncommonly long. Some teachers stayed in job for decades. The school paid well and the buildings were beautiful, as was Sweden on the ski trip organized for some years by the athletic director. To teach in this world was to live in it, part of each day at least. More important, teachers received a remission benefit for their own children, thereby positioning them, via Buckley, to attend an Ivy League college and law school, become an intern at the DA's office, a summer associate at Davis Polk, a clerk on the Third Circuit, full associate at Quinn Emanuel—whose website notes that "we have also obtained five 9-figure jury verdicts, forty-three 9-figure settlements, and nineteen 10-figure settlements"—and so, perhaps, send their own children to private school, at full price. I do not know what became of Sidoli's family, but this was the trajectory for the children of some other teachers, at least.

Sidoli's great nemesis on the faculty was a different sort of man, committed staunchly to strategy one, *insu-*

lation. He did not have children of his own and dedicated himself entirely, so far as we could tell, to us boys and our study of Latin. Fogarty was his name, and he was widely beloved, with his hooded eyes, gleaming comb-over, and uncontainable chest hair. No matter how tight the collar, it loosened as the day progressed, until wisps of grey and white and black sprang up beneath his Adam's apple. We called him "Wolfman Jack." Like Sidoli, Fogarty was white, middle-aged, and favored dark suits—but his were spotless, chalk-free. He was perhaps the most formal of our teachers, except in those moments when, sotto voce but to the whole class, he shielded his mouth with the back of a hand and relayed some scandalous bit of news: "McDonell, late again, *not* Hotchkiss material." It was one of many theatrical tricks with which he held our attention—but he seemed to lose control of it sometimes, turning on his fellow faculty and muttering perhaps that "*some* teachers are engaged in throwing chalk, and the headmaster certainly doesn't look kindly on that sort of behavior, I can tell you." His most famous classroom technique was "Roman Roulette," in which he called upon us at random for noun declensions—"*magister,* masculine, noun, meaning 'teacher' . . . us-i-o-orum-isque-ibus-it-is-ident, sir!" Failing to answer correctly, we were dubbed "dunce!" and obliged to sit beneath our desks for the remainder of the period, or until called upon again and able to redeem ourselves with a correct declension. Another of Fogarty's techniques was to order us, when one of us farted, to "positions!"—at which we fanned our notebooks and opened and closed the windows and door furiously until the odor passed. Swinging the door was the position of highest prestige, and Fogarty inevitably assigned it to the student who had suffered the severest humiliation during Roman Roulette. I think he may have borrowed "positions!" from our English teacher (or from a film?), a scion of one of the country's most famous publishing houses who had been teaching the definition of the appositive to wealthy twelve-year-olds for over a decade—"a noun or pronoun used to identify or describe another noun or pronoun, sir!" In our ignorant way—failing, then, to understand that there is no higher calling—we speculated as to why someone with so famous a name would be a *teacher*. Some fall from grace, perhaps, which none of us imagined for ourselves, to such a subservient profession. Fogarty, in contrast, we could imagine doing nothing else. On the day he died of cancer, after twenty-four years at Buckley, he wrote two letters: one to his priest, and one to the headmaster. The school paid for a notice in *The New York Times*.

I'm reluctant to dig any further into memory, to excavate, down in the school basement, the blue-aproned woodworking teacher who stopped us cutting our fingers off with the jigsaw and spoke in perfect, if perhaps unintentional, aphorisms: "First make a spoon, then we'll talk about a sword." Or any of the rest. Childhood often glows with nostalgia, and mine is additionally burnished by ongoing attention from the institutions that crafted it. Buckley's hundredth-anniversary gala was held at white-clothed tables around the Temple of Dendur, a two-thousand-year-old Egyptian shrine in the Metropolitan Museum of Art. As the speakers observed, neither the facilities nor the championships nor the capital campaign made the school great—its people did. They were right. In the end, you see, we loved these teachers, even the ones we hated. They were permanent features of our dreamy childhoods. They gave us the basics—"Mr. McDonell, there is *always* time to buckle your belt before leaving the lavatory"—and more, not least a love of reading. Many, like Fogarty, dedicated their lives to the school. And so, from the beginning, our love for *them* was tangled with love for *it*—and the *system* upon which it depended. Such immature, tangled love, which conflates people and institutions, tells us as much or more about the ruling class as decadence does. For *it,* rather than decadence, drove the endowment past $100 million, carrying strategies one, two, and three, like the *Niña, Pinta,* and *Santa Maria,* on an inevitable tide.

Our summer holidays were longer than the public schools' and many of us left the city every June. But our education did not stop, it only shifted focus. From six to fourteen, for example, June through August, I attended the Junior Yacht program at the Devon Yacht Club in

Amagansett, New York. The program divided us by age into Sandpipers, Optimists, and Seniors. Sandpipers were named for the small shorebird, Optimists for the eponymous one-person sailboat. These were about the size of bathtubs and we sailed them from the club's beach out onto Gardiners Bay, capsizing them, righting them, learning the skills and language of that tradition: *close-hauled, broad reach, run, tiller, halyard, keel*. Once we mastered the Optimist, at age eleven or so, we became Seniors and moved on to the 420. This was a dinghy, nearly fourteen feet long, with a jib and mainsail and even a setup for what is called a trapeze, which is a harness you clip to the rigging so you can stand on the edge of the hull as the boat *heels*—leans—in high wind. The lessons were in skill, but also—perhaps more so— in taste. For trapezing over whitecaps was but one of many pleasures imprinted on our psyches in those summers, so deeply as to become beloved, essential pastimes, elements of our very selves, which, at whatever cost, some of us would feel compelled to maintain for the rest of our lives.

The planks of the dock were warm under our feet and the day was divided: sailing, swimming, tennis, and lunch—arts and crafts only if it rained. For swimming we walked out along the pier, over seagull guano and the dried shells of spider crabs, dove off, swam laps back and forth to the pilings where the cormorants sat. The water was green and cold, the girls faster than the boys. On the clubhouse deck, grandmothers watched,

ate Caesar salad, patted their lips with crisp white nap-
kins, and planned to see each other again at "Family
Night."

This was every Thursday of the summer. The club
put out a buffet and hired a band. You had to wear a
jacket and tie and the rule was enforced. If you arrived
without, the maître d' provided a faded spare. The
band, Hot Wax, seemed to us ancient and played only
covers—the Isley Brothers' "Shout" was always their
finale. The dining room was open to the bay, its yellow
light spilling onto the cool sand and out over the water.
Hot Wax was audible down the beach, even past the
crumbling brick smokestack a mile or so east, which
served as our navigational landmark.

This smokestack was key to local history—all that
remained of a coal power plant constructed for Amagansett's first clutch of mansions. On a hunting trip in 1906,
a pair of businessmen from Ohio determined that the
area would make a fine summer enclave and established
the "Devon Colony." One of them was William Cooper Procter, whose grandfather had founded the con-
sumer goods company Procter & Gamble, which today
owns, among other brands, Ivory, Old Spice, Tampax,
Joy, Gillette, Oral-B, Crest, Charmin, Frédéric Fekkai,
and Mr. Clean. He and his hunting buddies apparently
founded the yacht club in 1908.

"A little bit softer now," sang Hot Wax, "a little bit
softer now, a little bit softer now . . ."

"Shout!" we all sang back, and danced in a circle.

Outside, Sandpipers made a prank of burying bowls of ice cream just beneath the sand, such that the adults might step in the mess. Lobster was served, steak, thick slices of tomato and mozzarella, iceberg lettuce. No money was ever exchanged at the club, no credit card ever seen. Everything was included in annual fees or charged after. At Family Night, or at lunch, or in the snack bar, you provided your member number: M-361, in my case. Then you'd fill out a chit with a small pencil, marking the grilled cheese or milkshake or burger or cheese fries that you wanted. Same for gas for your boat. Marina, kitchen, and wait staff all wore uniforms, white and blue, vaguely nautical, and were largely from Ireland. I don't remember ever seeing groundskeepers, but the club was immaculate, from the gravel to the dune grass to the clay tennis courts to the White Room. That was the name, I can't remember whether officially or not, of the lounge/bar in which every piece of furniture was white—like almost every person I ever saw at the club.

And every Fourth of July, fireworks. These were organized by George Plimpton, a longtime member, prominent writer and editor, and close friend of my parents. George was an honorary New York City fireworks commissioner and wore the title with some pride. For the Devon display he enlisted a famous firework family whose factory, one tragic year, exploded "up island." George once brought a troop of circus performers—trapeze artists and dwarves—to the club, and this was chuckled over. I can't remember where I heard all that, or rather, overheard it—it was part of the ambient grown-up noise. George also once, hypnotizingly, looked directly into my eyes and told me: Just as *I* was looking into *his* eyes, *he* had looked into the eyes of a man who had seen Pickett's Charge—the culminating action at the Battle of Gettysburg. This made me feel connected to something secret, old, and important—another club, inside the club.

And he beat me soundly at tennis. Even in his seventies, when I was an adolescent, he sent me running all over the court. I was not a particularly good tennis player. But I played tournaments at other clubs and achieved a certain, socially useful competence. We were all taught, at least, the rhyme:

Fifteen thirty forty game, every game is scored the same.

Many years later, tennis was a way to bond with a handful of English one percenters on Oxford's carefully trimmed grass. Between points, we talked about interesting legal cases or our ambitions to do good in Afghanistan. Versions of these conversations eventually arrived back at the yacht club via its speakers series, when a politician I knew from Kabul and London spoke there to raise awareness and money, to lobby whoever happened to be in the wicker chairs that lovely summer evening to stop the surge of troops. Other speakers spoke for other causes. At dusk afterward, a brass cannon was regularly rolled onto the deck and fired, and the flag was always carefully lowered and folded in the traditional way, as some children were shushed, while others stood with their hands over their hearts.

Over their heads, the view across the bay was of Gardiners Island, which is shaped like a conch shell. It is one of the largest and longest continuously held private islands in the country—colonized by the Gardiners in 1639 and in the family ever since. One of the heirs told *Newsday* in 2004, "We have always married into wealth. We've covered all our bets. We were on both sides of the Revolution, and both sides of the Civil War. The Gardiner family always came out on top." As Seniors, we were brought to visit, to see the endemic bird life and windmill, the graveyard and airstrip—then told sternly not to sneak onto the island, as teenagers sometimes did. This was a lesson, however, I did not learn. Instead, I stole, then hung in my bedroom, a heavy *No Trespassing* sign from the island's shore. It was an irresistible destination—the place where, in 1699, the privateer Captain Kidd had made a deal with Mr. Gardiner to bury treasure, stolen from an East India Company ship, which had been plying its usual trade in gold, and silver, and slaves.

Then, at the end of every summer, we returned to our more formal education. This, it's important to note, occurred not only in the classroom but also in the gym and on the playing fields. The school took physical education extremely seriously and encouraged competition. For example, once a week we began the day at the sports building in sweatpants and T-shirts rather than coats and ties. For the first half of the period we split up: football players to the matted fourth floor, soccer players to the hardwood first floor, and so on. During the period's second half, however, we were all brought together in the third-floor gymnasium. This was fully equipped for gymnastics: high bar, pommel horse, vault, parallel bars, rings, a spring-backed tumbling floor. Also a weight system and a pair of ropes that hung—tempting or terrifying, depending on your disposition—from the high ceiling. I recall my nerves walking in, for this second half of the period was dedicated to the dreaded PFI, *physical fitness index,* by which we were ranked—beginning, I think, age six.

The origins of the index were, like Quiet Street, obscure. Whether borrowed from some physiology lab or dastardly military program or simply invented by the sport-sirs, I never knew. It was a fairly complex system. One's PFI score was determined by a calculation of chin-ups, sit-ups, push-ups, standing broad jump, bench press, and rope-climbing time. Our self-reported numbers were taken very seriously. Misreporting them was an unthinkable breach of the honor code, and anyway would have required co-conspirators. One might begin at sit-ups, another boy holding your feet, or push-ups, with your partner's small fist on the floor beneath your chest. Your solar plexus had to touch his knuckles for a push-up to count, and we counted for each other.

"Three, two, one," a sport-sir would announce, "go!"

Or a whistle. And we'd do as many push-ups or

sit-ups as possible, or climb the rope, or broad jump for distance. Thereafter, our scores were used to rank and sort us into clubs. At the top was the Gladiator Club. Its requirements were sixty-five sit-ups in one minute, seventy-five push-ups in two minutes, fifteen chin-ups, and ten bench presses of 85 percent of your body weight. Gladiators were awarded a grey T-shirt emblazoned with a hulking blue weight lifter. A rank below was the Super Strength Club—their T-shirt was yellow with blue type. Then came the Strength Club, white with blue type. In the event you did not meet PFI requirements for even lowly Strength Club, you were not in any club at all and doomed to wear standard-issue blue.

Above all the clubs lay one, even higher, echelon of achievement: school record. These most auspicious of accomplishments were posted in the lobby beside the trophy case and the lesser, more volatile rankings and club memberships. I remember the awe and skepticism with which I looked at the chin-up record— forty-four!—set back in 1923. And I was very proud to be posted a Gladiator—though I intuited that what pleasure I took in my accomplishment had its inverse among classmates who never made it up the rope.

Wherever we landed in the rankings, we were encouraged to be "hard-nosed." The phrase was a favorite of our football coach, Mr. Trauth Jr., whose father, Mr. Trauth Sr., had also taught at the school— boxing, before the sport was abandoned in 1980.

Mr. Trauth Jr. also coached wrestling and baseball, for thirty-one years.

"Losers make excuses" was another of his phrases, "winners make commitments."

And Mr. Trauth Jr. was a winner. He coached us to astonishing, record-breaking, dynastic winning streaks in football, and even more so wrestling—131 matches—a sport in which his pedagogy was unorthodox and legendary. He used, for example, a striking analogy to teach us the maneuver known as "the cradle." Down on the mat, he would demonstrate on some unlucky soul: "You bring your hand around behind his n-n-neck-k-k, like it's the Red Army landing behind the lines, in enemy territory. Then . . . *wham*," and he would execute the final lock. "You got 'em."

Mr. Trauth Jr. had a moderate stutter, and awkward tension sometimes arose as we waited for him to get through his plosives and hard consonants. Once, receiving a stuttered reprimand, a boy became notorious for responding, "Well, sir, that's easy for *you* to say." Trauth Jr. ignored the comment, but: the audacity of that boy! Because Trauth Jr. was fearsome. We knew his strength: He *always* got down on the mat with us to demonstrate, even though he appeared to be the oldest of our coaches, stubble grey and white across the deep lines of his face. And when, around the age of ten or eleven, another boy bullied me for a few months, Trauth Jr. had some very old and specific advice.

He called me into the athletic office, known as "the

bull pen." The senior coaches all had desks in there, bantered with each other from their swivel chairs, lords of our tiny universe.

"So, Nicky, you're having some trouble with Todd," Trauth Jr. observed.

I can't remember the exchange precisely, but I agreed.

"The next time he gives you a hard time"—Trauth Jr. held up a fist—"you s-s-sock him in the nose."

This, however, I did not do. Instead, I kicked Todd's football helmet under a parked bus and was rightly mocked for it. But the spell of bullying passed, Todd and I became friendly, and Trauth Jr. taught another class of boys, many of whom carried themselves with unusual physical confidence, instilled by his lessons. Others with whom I've spoken while writing this book say they connect the intense competition encouraged by Trauth Jr. and PFI to adult anxiety and shame—at being overweight, or otherwise low on the index.

Between Devon and Buckley, sailing, homework, PFI, and all the sports, our childhoods were strictly scheduled and managed. Still, there was some idle time in which to get into trouble. It was a grotesque but unoriginal feature of my cohort that our rebellion, at the very top of the economic pyramid, was to mimic people at the very bottom—or an idea of them, anyway. Some of the boys I went to school with, and many more in Manhattan's private school universe, adopted the tics and language of Blackness, as they imagined it. They aspired to become "prep school gangsters." *You got sonned!* they'd say, and were each other's *dawg.* In puffy North Face coats, they *tagged* the Upper East and West Sides with paint pens. Released from football practice, they'd take off their ties and become a *crew,* signing the crew's name, for example, on the side door of the Duane Reade pharmacy a few blocks from the school. BHS—the Buckley Hood Squad—was one. They threw invented gang signs, or real ones, crooking their fingers to spell "blood" at each other across the risers at Glee Club rehearsal. Like all children, they knew instinctively how to get their parents' attention, what behavior was surest to agitate.

I was often, myself, an idiot adolescent. But I was not one of these prep school gangsters. They seemed to me obviously unkind—I didn't like how their leaders tended to bully the less able members of our class. I don't, and didn't, know what they were thinking. I suspect they weren't, that they were engaged instead in a kind of thoughtless play, as with matches, or the smashing of spider crabs at the seashore. Still, a child *knows* that matches are dangerous—and that taking life, no matter its form, is consequential and, wantonly done, *bad.* My peers knew, on some level, that imitating their idea of Black people was wrong. To commit an immoral act is not to *be* immoral, of course, and we were young. But we were not, by then, children. I once saw Afghan soldiers who appeared as young, perhaps fifteen years old, in Helmand. And they, who were responsible for actual lives, were mentally and physically the same as us—and the Black teenagers my peers imitated—despite our vastly different material circumstances. I think the impulse to dismiss this reality as naïve or obvious shares a root with the more wanton impulse to smash crabs or mimic, mockingly, people of another race. The shared root, which I recognize in myself, is fear. I often thought the behavior of the prep school gangsters stemmed, in part, from anxious lives at home. And being anxious all the time, they were perhaps more prone to fear white America's historical *other*—Black people—and so mimed a fantasy of them, to hide their fear and raise themselves up, in a tradition of evil violence that they did not understand.

In any case, by the time they graduated high school, most had realized that prep school gangsterdom was at the least socially unacceptable. When in later years it came up in conversation, it was treated lightly—as folly or phase, a harmless identity quickly shed—rather than the manifestation of deeper pathologies, which we all shared, and which, always, eventually, surfaced and spread poison.

I remember, in my own case, for example, a particular day in high school. For three years after Buckley, before college, I attended the Riverdale Country School. It was less rarefied than Buckley, though equally expensive, coed, more liberal. At Buckley we met Republican senator Strom Thurmond; at Riverdale, it was Democrat Chuck Schumer. The campus sprawled over twenty-odd acres in one of the Bronx's whitest, priciest neighborhoods, shaded by old trees. Early in my time there, an Indian American girl, Trina, sat down beside me in philosophy class and we became fast friends—both being, as we were, bookish, smart-alecky flirts. Among Trina's many appealing qualities was the possession of a driver's license, and one afternoon she tooled us around her hometown in northern New Jersey, introducing me to trip hop (Massive Attack), sentimental indie (Belle and Sebastian), and the suburbs, about which I knew nothing, living as I did in Manhattan or, during summers, the resort villages to the east. Her father, who had emigrated from India, was our physics teacher, and Trina attended Riverdale at a major discount. Since she couldn't afford the designer clothes that most of our classmates wore, she'd committed early in high school to a uniform of her father's old pants—they both had a twenty-nine-inch waistline—and five-dollar vintage T-shirts. I didn't know this at the time. I just thought she was cool. And she was: knowing where I was earnest, shrewd where I was naïve. She smoked with a ferocious teenage nonchalance and tried in vain to correct my own technique. We had some predictable romantic tension. Not so long after we'd become friends, she drank two and a half forties and declared a crush on me.

I wasn't attracted to her and didn't want to make out. Trina promptly got over it and introduced me to her friends, who became my friends. When I was a junior, she cemented these relationships by inviting me to join her clique on their senior spring break in Paris—the "alternative" answer to the Bahamas, where the preppier kids went. We stayed in tiny hotels and confided in each other about our families. We talked about Mos Def and Kant and, more credibly, what it meant to be emo. We had been friends for over a year when, to my complete surprise, she slapped me hard across the face.

With the exception of my younger brother and a quickly fired nanny, this was the first time anyone had ever really hit me. I had no idea what I'd done.

"How do you think it makes me feel," she demanded, her eyes shining, "to have my best friend call me a darkie all the time?"

I'd never considered the question. I knew the word was taboo but had taken to using it, making jokes about "the jungle," imitating her father's accent. My parents, if they'd caught me, would have told me off severely. But by my warped logic it was okay, harmless—funny, even—to make jokes like this, because Trina didn't care. Or so I thought, even though she'd *told me,* more than once, not to say the word. I thought I was flirting with her, mocking *the rules*—one of the things we liked to do best. I remember the sting in my cheek. But I can't remember, really, what I thought or felt in that moment except a sense of surprise, and this: that the word was a deal-breaker in our friendship, and that if I wanted to be friends with Trina, I was going to have to stop using it. All the baggage, all the history, whether I was racist—I didn't think about any of that till after, some of it not for years. I just reacted to her—the look on her face, in her eyes. I didn't want to lose her. I apologized and never used the word again.

Thereafter she teased me about the episode sometimes, but didn't hold it over my head. We remained close, got closer. One summer, we lived for a month in my mother's vacant Upper East Side apartment with my college roommate and younger brother. When I brought her to the Devon Yacht Club, she made typically accurate and hilarious observations, which I wish I could now recall. (Assessing a draft of this book, less hilariously to my mind, she said with a shrug, "Sarcastic, dark insider's view of privilege"). As years passed, she told me more about what it was like to be not white and not rich at that school and in that community. I don't think either of us would have guessed, senior year, that one day I'd be master of ceremonies at her wedding. We became a kind of family.

But in lucid moments I remember: This is how one percenters think, are conditioned to think. We think life is easier, fairer, more resolved than it actually is. We often miss what is self-evident. Plenty of one percenters got slapped, one way or another, and forgiven. In fact, we were forgiven constantly throughout our youths. And our transgressions were cumulative, more consequential than we cared to understand—but mostly, we paid no price. Instead, we went to college.

Quiet Street ran straight through Harvard. I applied early and was accepted. My new friends skewed foreign and midwestern and not so rich, but I remained close to some one percenters, and aware of many. They made up about 20 percent of the student body.

In many ways, the rich experienced Harvard like everyone else. Everyone had to take the "core curriculum"—a class each in quantitative reasoning, literature, several other fundamental disciplines. For moral reasoning, for example, I took a class, still taught, called "If There Is No God, All Is Permitted," in wood-paneled Sanders Theatre. For physical science, "Observing the Sun and Stars," up in the observatory. Everyone lived in Harvard Yard as freshmen, was invited to tea at eighteenth-century clapboard faculty houses, endured the snowy Cambridge winters, used the same vast libraries.

The one percent, nonetheless, had a different college experience. The starkest symbols of the difference were the "final clubs." These eight social organizations were all-male, dated from the eighteenth and nineteenth centuries, and owned clubhouses off campus. But the off-campus/on-campus line was very thin. The mascot of the most exclusive club—a pig—was carved into one of the stone arches above an entrance to Harvard Yard. I was "punched" by that one, the Porcellian, possibly at the request of George, the writer I mentioned earlier, who was himself a member. I attended two "punch" events, essentially social auditions.

The first was held near Harvard Yard in a large town house. Open bars catered to a room of sophomores trying to make good impressions on juniors and seniors, all in coats and ties. You could feel the tension, how high the stakes for some, in every exchange of *oh yeah, I went to Hotchkiss with his brother!* I remember the thick carpets and asking a member in a pin-striped suit about the green-and-white club lapel pin he wore.

"That's cool, what's that?" I asked, without thinking.

He replied with disdain—"It's just something we do"—as though he didn't want to talk about it. I soon got the sense that mentioning the accessories and symbols of the ritual we were enacting was frowned upon. Pin man left me in the crowd.

I was invited back, though, for a second event. On a cold Sunday morning a few weeks later, a chartered bus brought us—the survivors of that first event—to a rolling estate somewhere outside Boston. Uniformed waiters served Bloody Marys off silver trays through a steak brunch. I didn't enjoy the touch football game, kept to myself, charmed no one, and wasn't invited to a third event. Years later, a member of the club—son of a cop, scholarship student, an exception—told me that I "didn't seem like [I] wanted to be there."

He was partly right. I never intended to join. But I attended those events, and one party at a less exclusive club, out of respect for George and curiosity born of the clubs' mystique. Legend had it, for example, that the Porcellian would give you a million dollars if you had not made your own million by age thirty. The reality was more banal—but also sometimes horrible. In a 2016 report commissioned by the university, a Task Force on the Prevention of Sexual Assault concluded that "while Final Clubs are not the exclusive or even the principal cause of sexual assault at the College, we also do not see any solution that does not involve addressing the disturbing practical and cultural implications they present in undergraduate life."

The one club party I attended was held nearly a decade before that report, the winter following my senior year, on Super Tuesday, 2008. I was reporting on the presidential race for a French magazine and had come back to campus thinking I'd find a useful scene for the article. Alumni often visited the clubs, and sometimes attended the parties. This one was marked by the arrival of the hotel heiress Paris Hilton, now famous for her DJ sets and child abuse advocacy, then for her leaked sex tape. The *Harvard Lampoon*—the college humor magazine—was awarding her a "Woman of the Year" prize, and she'd come to campus to accept. I saw her at around three in the morning. At one point, she draped herself over a student next to me, a big, gentle actor whose father sat on the board of a tobacco company. He looked embarrassed. Pressed close in the crowd, I asked Paris if she'd voted.

"It's so complicated," she told me.

"But who would you vote for, if you had voted?"

"I don't know . . ."

"Maybe Obama?"

"Yeah. He's the coolest of them, isn't he?"

She was playing the role for which she is best known. Her attention soon went to some other young man.

That club, the Spee, elected in 2015 to admit women—but this was exceptional. The clubs were not legally part of the university, and thus wrote their own rules. When I was a student, freshmen women often waited in line, in the snow, in miniskirts, for judgment from the male members and so, perhaps, admittance to a party. After the sexual assault task force published its report, Harvard took steps to force gender integration. In 2016, it announced sanctions against uncooperative clubs. The sanctions would bar members from sports team captaincies, certain prestigious scholarships, and the like. In response, a group of clubs brought two lawsuits against the university, alleging discrimination. In federal court, the presiding judge—Dartmouth '60, Columbia Law '66—rejected Harvard's bid to dismiss the case. Noting the "prevailing interpretation of federal law," Harvard soon rescinded the sanctions. Under increased scrutiny, some of the clubs issued statements claiming to have become more diverse. The last I saw of Ms. Hilton, she was being carried aloft by a scrum of members through a landscape of leather furniture, deeper into the club, past a stuffed bear that roared up on its hind legs as though defending itself, or perhaps its cubs, from some danger.

Taxidermy, come to think of it, appeared with quite startling frequency inside The Bubble. Dead animals on the wall suggested intimacy and environmentalism rather than bloodlust, exclusivity, and colonialism. That "nerds" or "haters" might dislike the bear was sad for *them*. Like the clubs, hunting itself was mostly for men. But "the girls" joined in as well, or at least came along for the weekend. Stags in Scotland, quail in Georgia, bonefish in the Bahamian flats. I knew two women who liked to recount how, following their first fox hunts—one in France, the other in England—they had been "blooded," the blood literally smeared on their high, pale cheekbones. Much was made of respect for the natural world, on the one percent's frequent holidays.

These holidays began long before college and were miraculous gifts. They recharged us, gave us new dreams, probably increased our life expectancies. And just as the one percent claimed to embrace diversity— through donations, scholarships—it claimed, through these trips, to embrace environmentalism, even as we were also, all the time, knowingly making the planet less hospitable to human life. The melancholy aspect of the stuffed bears was appropriate. They had a lot to be sad about; in a certain light, they were talismans of an incoherent and clueless death cult. Once, on a reporting trip to Medellín, at lunch with the sister of murderous narco-tycoon El Chapo, I noticed in the corner a stuffed baby hippopotamus. "Above all," she told me, "my brother was a conservationist." The elite degraded the environment and simultaneously spent money to save it, donating for access.

My most memorable holiday of this sort was to the Galápagos Islands. The density of biomass was stunning. I watched albatrosses raise their wings, shuffle to cliff's edge, dive off. They were so massive that this was a handy way to get airborne and out to sea—where they might stay for months, according to our local guides, who had been hired by the venerable, originally Scandinavian expedition company. The expedition leaders were white Americans, the guides Ecuadorian doctoral candidates in zoology. The boat had been chartered by an oil family that liked to talk politics. The patriarch told me over his tequila on the aft deck, "I don't trust any government that doesn't trust me to have whatever kind of weapon I want." The logic was more convincing on his boat. Snorkeling with his children, I saw penguins shoot past like minor but ancient gods, terns dive down through clear water, streaks of bubbles racing heavenward. The water was silver with fish, with so many seabirds diving at once that we were swimming in a froth. Above, frigatebirds attacked and robbed each other in midair. When we crossed the equator, one guide dressed up as a pirate and put the children through a mock "line-crossing ceremony," a shipboard ritual dating to whale-hunting expeditions in which sailors crossing the equator for the first time were hazed. The kids, if I recall, were squirted with a water gun and made to hop, giggling, over a line on the deck.

And everywhere we went on the islands, as guides explained the rare wildlife, the patriarch joked, "Hmm, that looks tasty, turtle soup!" Or, "A little blue-footed booby fricassee?" And so on. Toward trip's end he said that he was in fact interested in *hunting* on the Galá-pagos Islands, and how could we make that happen? The guides thought he was joking, realized he wasn't, and came up with a plan. It would be too difficult to circumvent Ecuadorian regulations with regard to hunting the islands *on foot*—the delicate ecosystem had to be protected. But from the air, it was perhaps pos-sible. Among the animals of the islands, goats were not endemic, having been introduced centuries prior by whalers. And so the guides suggested hunting in the Galápagos Islands by rifle, from helicopter, for goats.

No goat hunting transpired, but not, I think, because the plan was too outrageous. Members of this oil family had been engaged, for many hundreds of millions of dollars, in other schemes that defied rea-son. One of them, for example, had financed a giant climate-controlled dome in the desert—to test the fea-sibility of life in space, since we were destroying it here on Earth.

———

Such trips and follies were too expensive for anyone but one percenters to undertake. They cost more than the plane tickets, the boat, the gas, the expedition fee. There were other prices, vast costs—genocide, rape, pillage—borne by whole other communities that, by the end of their educations, one percenters knew about but often ignored or spun to their advantage. Thus a white family not only kept a boat to ferry guests to its camp on an island off the coast of Kenya, it employed a Maasai guy who had been living there, taking care of the place "since Grandfather."

"We live outside when we're here, just like them," the mistress of the camp told me.

I was, in that instance, visiting from a bigger island, Lamu, to which I'd traveled following two months reporting in Rwanda and Ethiopia. I was twenty-two and had recently graduated from college. It seemed very reasonable to check into one of Lamu's most expensive hotels, the Peponi, for a month—so long as I wrote another novel in that month. I did, barely, based on the reporting I'd just finished. And at the bar one evening, watching the sun set over the Indian Ocean, I met the mistress of that camp. She'd been raised, partly, in the Maasai community, into which her anthropologist mother had married. The story was more nuanced than I understood, then or now, and I didn't capture enough nuance in the novel. But I also met a movie producer at that bar who bought the rights to that novel then and there, which made staying in that colonial-chic hotel, expensive as it was, profitable.

Such were the people in The Bubble. And if here, finally, your mind rebels against generalization—"we," "The Bubble"—as mine often does, please consider the possibility that such methodological risks can be generous, and should sometimes be taken on account of the urgency of the situation, in which eighty million people control 38 percent of all household wealth, four billion people control less than 2 percent, and inequality is rising, and correlates with authoritarianism, and civil war. The one percent, of course, would be well prepared for that catastrophe, no matter how clueless it sometimes seems. For there is internal logic to the decadence, an intuitive calculus that pays off, even if you don't know how, exactly, until someone buys the rights, or writes the letter, or offers you their mansion for the week. The house is empty anyway, they might say, so please, go ahead, take the kids, don't mention it.

II

A bove all, the one percent maintained a monopoly on violence. Though I walked at its knee, I did not recognize its nakedness until I became a foreign correspondent in Iraq. I was twenty-five and a reporter for *Time* magazine, embedding with the U.S. Army's 1st Cavalry Division in Mosul. On that trip I stayed initially on Combat Outpost Hotel, which lay in the shadow of an abandoned hotel tower on the banks of the Tigris and consisted of the usual sandbags, razor wire, and trailers where the soldiers slept. Mortars were a threat—a blessed dud had recently punched a hole through the roof of one of the trailers—and so on arrival I asked a lieutenant why he and his men didn't move their outpost *inside* the hotel. He informed me that the Navy SEALs already occupied it, and so no one else was allowed. He agreed this was stupid, but such was life for a young officer, and therefore his reporter charge, in Iraq. I nursed, in the following days, some hard feelings toward the Navy SEALs, and hierarchies in general. Getting mortared when we could have been inside the hotel would have been a particularly need-

less way to die in that needless war. So I was not dis-
pleased when, later that week, I was moved to a combat
outpost located within the reassuringly thick walls of
the summer palace of one of Saddam Hussein's daughters. After that, I did not think about Combat Outpost
Hotel for several months—and might never have again,
had I not received that spring an invitation from my
old school, Buckley. A fellow alumnus I had grown
up with was to speak at Friday assembly on his experience as a Navy SEAL in Iraq. Not having been back to
Buckley since I was a child, I accepted the invitation.

On the morning of the assembly, from the warm,
dim mezzanine, I watched the SEAL's presentation
with feelings of nostalgia and expanding dread. He
paced the varnished stage in a pin-striped suit, deliv-
ering a combination of amusing anecdotes and sentimental generalities about military life and his Iraq tour
as he clicked through a slideshow. Without a hitch,
he evaded the question from a hypnotized child about
what it was like to kill someone: "Some things it's
better not to talk about." And one of the pictures in
his slideshow, I was surprised to see, was of the hotel
tower beside Combat Outpost Hotel. He and his fellow
SEALs had lived on the top floor.

As a student, I'd looked up to this SEAL. He'd been
a formidable athlete, a fellow Gladiator, and though we
were never friends, we were friendly. Walking south
past Park Avenue's blooming tulips post-assembly, we
agreed that we might well have been at Combat Out-

post Hotel at the same time—he inside, fighting the war, I outside, reporting on it. After a few blocks we went our separate ways. The SEAL had by then been honorably discharged and was embarking upon a career in "energy services." That day he seemed in a hurry.

Such noblesse oblige operators, no fools, tended to discretion and the maintenance of a powerful idea: Soldiering was a meritocratic, perhaps the most meritocratic, vocation. This idea dated, maybe apocryphally, to Homer—"The first in valour, as the first in place." In the military, even elites were obliged to get down in the mud with everyone else, endure hazing and occasionally brutal training, enact rituals. All were part of the very old tradition by which states turned civilians into soldiers, breaking down their identities so they would kill and, if necessary, die. Definitely, on the front line of the invasions, the rich were in danger like everyone else.

And yet every rich person I knew who joined the military had an extraordinary career: led an elite unit, saw combat, served with distinction, worked with generals, received commendations, and so on. I've also encountered one percenters at the DOJ, FBI, CIA, and NYPD, all of whom inspired or recruited others from their tribe. In this way, the one percent maintained cultural ties to—as well as financial and political control of—the apparatuses of state violence. This violent monopoly underlay every profession a member of the ruling class might consider as he or she embarked on a career. The Bubble hardened, in adulthood, into an apparently invincible Fortress.

Among my peers, the most common career was finance. The *Harvard Crimson* reported that in the graduating class of 2007, 47 percent of students entering the workforce went into financial services or consulting. I suspect the number was equal or higher for one percenters. Whether investment banking, asset management, or private equity, however, few one percenters I knew seemed to enjoy the actual business of decks and spreadsheets. They liked their colleagues. They liked flying first class. They liked the deal-making culture. Still, they didn't seem very happy. FOMO—fear of missing out—was rampant, driving them to co-opt or invade one subculture after another during their compressed, often narcotically enhanced holidays. The leisure was manic because the work was relentless. And in this context, the pandemic, for many rich people I knew, was a relief. It allowed them to dispense entirely with the trappings of normalcy—schedule, commute, office—and settle into country houses, much like aristocrats of previous centuries.

The one percenters who did not enter finance went instead into medicine, politics, tech, education, the arts. Rich graduates had more freedom to choose—though as it turned out, quite a few of them ended up after a few years, like the SEAL, going into finance or tech or corporate law as well. Journalists became lawyers, artists became fund associates, aid workers became real estate investors. At apex, all the jobs were similar—wield and maintain power—even if they didn't seem so on the ride up.

I spent some time, for example, in the art world, attending gallery openings, artist dinners, dropping by cool white spaces in the afternoon. It was a great pleasure to walk through nondescript Chelsea doors into a world of promiscuous, aesthetically concerned youth, and the striking objects in which they traded. Perhaps more than other industries, the art world attracted one percenters with a subversive, or at least ninety-nine-percent-curious, streak. Overtly political, bite-the-hand pieces were common. But art galleries were only "open to the public" in such a way that they could provide free booze that never ran out. One had to know where to go. Inside, the art market was freely discussed in terms of money laundering and tax evasion—even as famous gallerists were occasionally sent to prison. A safer way to succeed in the business was by launching a gallery in empty family real estate. I saw this once in a West Village residential development that was awaiting tenants. The gallerists had hung the art in apartments that soon bankers would lease. Whether the works themselves were good investments, tax write-offs, or playthings—ideally all three—the real estate was serving an extra purpose inside the family portfolio, even while it was vacant: jump-starting the young dealer's career. She didn't have to worry about making rent, could focus on the art, take her time—and so was more likely to succeed. Such dealers tended to play down their advantage.

In this, elite art dealers resembled elites in other professions—especially politics. Donald Trump was the preeminent example. Though he received over $413 million in loans from his father, he presented himself as a self-made man. "I got a very, very small loan from my father many years ago," he said at a 2016 news conference. "I built that into a massive empire. And I paid my father back that loan." Many politicians refrained from such bald lies but omitted and spun to dissociate themselves from the one percent. Trey Hollingsworth, Republican congressman from Indiana, founded the industrial real estate company Hollingsworth Capital Partners with his multimillionaire father and had a net worth of some $50 million. "A small business owner," his website biography read, "Trey began renovating and rehabilitating abandoned industrial sites after graduating from business school."

Like Hollingsworth, the majority of men and women in the 116th Congress were millionaires. To hear them speak was to get the impression that all were self-made. I rarely read or saw any address their own wealth or its consequences. Elise Stefanik, the youngest Republican woman ever elected to Congress, represented, she claimed, "everyday Americans." Stefanik attended a private day school, the Albany Academy for

Girls, which regularly sent students to the Ivy League. When she spoke at the Republican National Convention, she mentioned that she was the first person in her immediate family to graduate from college, but not that the college was Harvard. When we met there as students, she was a government major in Winthrop House serving as vice president at the Institute of Politics, on her way to work in the Bush administration. A few years later, at a mutual friend's wedding, I watched her put on a MAGA cap and mock Trump. This was before he was considered a serious contender. Stefanik would eventually sacrifice her integrity in defense of his fraudulent claims about the 2020 election. Her father owned Premium Plywood Products Inc., which according to its website, had been "distributing the highest quality hardwood plywood and products" throughout the Northeast for over twenty years.

The journalists covering politics were also often one percenters. Fox News anchor Tucker Carlson attended St. George's in Rhode Island, a prep school fed, now and then, by Buckley. His father served as an ambassador to the Seychelles and director of the Voice of America. His stepmother was an heir to the Swanson food company. As an adult, Carlson too presented himself as defender of "everyday Americans," launching lunatic tirades against the ruling class. Carlson was an avatar of the elite's worst, most cynical elements.

More reasonable news organizations than Carlson's were dominated by one percenters too. CNN's advertising slogan was "The Most Trusted Name in News." The network's star anchor, Anderson Cooper, was a Vanderbilt. Here is the network's chief international correspondent, Clarissa Ward—whom I like and met in Kabul—in her memoir *On All Fronts,* on how she got her own start:

> One advantage I did have over other contenders in my search for an entry-level journalism job was my facility with languages. Since my first French lessons at age eight, languages just made sense to me. By now, I spoke French and Italian, as well as basic Spanish and Russian. In the end, though, it was my mother's savvy and a routine visit to the dentist that led to my first gig in journalism. By a stroke of serendipity, my mother's dentist in Palm Beach was also the dentist of CNN's Moscow bureau chief, Jill Dougherty. I was introduced to Dougherty and then was overjoyed to be offered an unpaid internship with CNN in Moscow, beginning in September.

Imagine the effect of this paragraph on an aspiring journalist who is neither rich nor connected.

I entered journalism in a similar way. After the publication of my first novel (more on which later), an editor at *Time,* whom my father knew, hired me as an intern in the magazine's Hong Kong bureau. My father, himself a magazine editor, would later hire *him* at *Sports Illustrated*. I've since helped a daughter of that editor try to place *her* college essay in *Teen Vogue*, whose editor *I* knew. And so on. Members of the one percent cultivated this network throughout their careers. It didn't just help with the first job; it helped with the last, and each between. Especially if you liked to switch industries, as many did. The managing editor of *Time*—which sent me to Combat Outpost Hotel— would, for example, later join the State Department as undersecretary for public diplomacy and public affairs. That particular move, journalism into "strategic communications," lay in a proud tradition. Even George Orwell, for example, produced propaganda for the BBC against the Third Reich. *Time*'s top editor was tasked to do likewise against ISIS with a distinguished, if not Orwellian, career behind him. But ISIS was not the Third Reich—it was a consequence of the U.S. invasion of Iraq and tolerance of Sunni persecution; and Orwell did not go on to tech-giant advisership like the undersecretary did, passing through the "revolving door" between journalism, government, tech, and academia.

Academia was, like politics and journalism, dense with one percenters from both left and right. As adjuncts and associates, they dedicated mental space to research that others had to use for rent and, networked before arrival, became full professors relatively quickly.

At Oxford, where I went to graduate school, exhila-
rating work was under way in every discipline I ever
heard anything about. I was especially taken with the
breakdown between the humanities and sciences, the
marriage of neuroscience, sociology, and evolutionary biology into explanations for human behavior. As
a master's student, I studied international relations and,
alarmingly, began to doubt free will. (Schopenhauer:
"One can choose what to do, but not what to want.")
My cohort was small. While several students attended
on Rhodes and Clarendon scholarships, it seemed like
most paid full fare. They were in their mid- to late
twenties and had already distinguished themselves for
their ambition, brains, success, and, in some cases,
arrogance.

I regret my own, at the time. I'd initially applied
to the university after a stint reporting in Sudan, seized
by the idea of *doing* rather than reporting. A false distinction, but one I then believed. I hoped that graduate studies might help me get a job as an aid worker or
even diplomat. My first application was rejected, but
I applied again the following year, from Afghanistan.
This time, I received a phone call from the program
director. She asked me if I was serious about the program, because there were people who really were, and
she didn't want to give me a place if I wasn't.

I promised diligence and, some weeks later,
received a letter of acceptance. I had by that time
become thoughtful enough to appreciate the privilege

of study and dedicated myself to research in the quietest library I could find. This was the Codrington, named for its original benefactor, Christopher Codrington, whose family fortune derived from sugar plantations and Caribbean slave labor. In consideration of that history, the Codrington was eventually renamed All Souls College Library. Its exterior was Gothic, its interior neoclassical. High windows cast their light on black marble; thousands of books filled the air with their old scent. It was a humbling place, officially reserved for members of the college or scholars who required its particular collections. I wasn't and didn't, but asked my adviser to write a letter to get me in and then wrote my thesis, on nomadism in international relations, at the library's dark tables. Upon its completion, I was obliged to make a formal verbal defense before a trio of professors clad in academic black tie. My defense went smoothly—so smoothly that at its conclusion, the professors offered me a place on the doctoral program to expand my thesis into a book. And here I cringe to remember myself, a younger one percenter. I declined the offer then and there, in the room. I did so for two reasons. First, I was eager to get a television show I was working on, about Afghanistan, on air. Second, I believed I could write and publish a nomad book without the support of the university and therefore, if I wanted, return to academia. Wasn't that the point of a doctorate, I thought, to get a book published? I could do that on my own; what other credential would

I need? I did not take seriously the professors' surprise, or their advice that I at least *think* about the opportunity, as it was very serious and would not come again.

They were right, of course. I got the television show running—but not for long. I published the nomad book to strong reviews—but this did not win me a job offer in academia. In fact, when I applied to the doctoral program after the TV show was canceled, I was rejected. Professors told me: We warned you. But I behaved, at twenty-eight, as if such opportunities would always be available. The arrogance was my own but inseparable from an education and career which to that point had indicated, always: Everything is possible. I cannot now imagine turning down such an opportunity so carelessly. To do so seems in retrospect as spoiled as a prep schooler kicking over a garbage can on Park Avenue.

Less subtle sorts of carelessness persisted at Oxford as well. One scion I met, of a Chinese political family, became famous for his sports cars and lavish parties but failed his exams. Rumor had it the university was going to expel him—until the British Foreign and Commonwealth Office intervened in consideration of diplomatic relations with China. The scion's father and mother were later arrested and separately convicted, the father for bribery, the mother on murder charges that many have speculated were politically motivated.

At Columbia Law School a few years later, shortly before he went into finance and Canadian exile, the scion told me he wanted to make a TV show like *Game of Thrones,* but about geopolitics. He wanted to go to Hollywood.

One percenters dominated that business too. They were excellent fantasists. That their fantasies exerted such power over the American psyche would have been laughable had the consequences not been so dire. Inevitably, the fantasies crept off location. Once, in the company and on the tab of two producers, an untrained AK–47-toting guard, and an uneasy screenwriter, I visited the city of Garissa, in eastern Kenya, to advise on a film based on my third novel. This "research" trip was, from a business point of view, superfluous. With his large, expensive camera, the lead producer/financier and his dopey guard attracted a great deal of attention in the market we visited: A clutch of young men evil-eyed them, went so far as to warn that taking pictures was *haram*. Mild stuff, but which could've escalated. Indeed, the Kenyan fixer we had retained, who had been warning the producer to be more discreet, fled nervously. My own shopping concluded, I followed. The screenwriter had long since decided to wait in the car with the doors locked. The lead producer escaped the wrath of the growing crowd, but I wouldn't have been surprised to see him get into a fight. When I confronted him about his behavior, he rebuffed me: "I've lived in Africa for years!"

In fact, he had a house in Lamu—where we'd met at the bar of that colonial-chic hotel and he'd bought the rights to my novel. He split his time between there, London, and Los Angeles. As I chewed qat that evening, it seemed funny, then not so funny—we all had four more days together. Our hotel, however, suffered brownouts and was not to the producers' taste. They decided to cut the trip short and have a plane return for us in the morning. Flying back to the coast, the pilot dipped our wings over the treetops. We flew very low, low enough to see, just for a moment, the faces of people in a village.

The movie remains in development. Such massive, wasteful spending was normal. I saw the same again in Morocco, on the production side, working on a show set in Afghanistan. Parts of the crew stayed in the best hotels, flew business class, drank a lot of tequila. A drama unto itself, with its own language. Our line producer favored two constructions: "a world where x" and "the x of it all." For example: "Is there a world where we wrap by midnight?" or "Let's figure out the Kenitra of it all."

Kenitra, a small port city in western Morocco, was our stand-in for Kabul. The "Kenitra of it all" involved, among other things, managing the crowd that inevitably gathered to watch the shoot—mistakenly believing, we eventually learned, that our lead was Tom Cruise, who was then shooting *Mission: Impossible—Rogue Nation,* at twenty times our budget, elsewhere in

Morocco. We producers talked about how welcoming this crowd was, even though the local kids stole props and, one day, while the fires of our fake car bomb were burning, a heavyset gentleman shouted (I paraphrase): *You American assholes! You come around and make us all look like terrorists, in this quiet neighborhood!* Seven million dollars later, the episode tested badly and was shelved, never to be broadcast. The project, my agents told me, was good for my career.

Soldiering, finance, art, politics, academia, show business—whatever the profession, one percenters were disproportionately successful. Immense confidence was both cause and consequence, reinforced by good dentists, education, networks, and so on. And yet for all our confidence, we didn't like to leave The Fortress, let alone confront the injustices that were becoming ever more apparent outside its walls.

Some of us promised to do so, just not quite yet. A friend explained to me that if he could only make ten million dollars in financial technology, or "fintech," that would be enough—he'd go to work on green energy and campaign finance reform. This was a friend who, like many, adored, even fetishized, data. Data was the commodity distinguishing elites born after 1980 or thereabouts from their predecessors. Our age famously valorized its data barons as much, perhaps more, as did previous ages their magnates, statesmen, and revolutionaries. The one percent, which knew these men best, was fully seduced, even as it often forbade its children from using the relevant technologies. Like many in my college class, I sometimes found it useful to mention that I had met Mark Zuckerberg, founder of Facebook, when we were freshmen, thereby establishing my proximity to power. This tendency, of which I was not proud, was not mine alone. It felt good to be close to power. Such good feeling discouraged evidence-based discussions of wealth, poverty, exploitation, and transformation. Even among those who—like my fintech friend, and Zuckerberg—knew the value of data.

Probably the world's most detailed historical data set on wealth (which I drew on in the preface) has been compiled by a French economist, Thomas Piketty, and his team. Piketty's books have sold millions of copies. He's been invited to speak at the most august institutions, reviewed in the *Wall Street Journal* as well as academic journals. His methods have been taken seriously by critics and peers. In his book *Capital and Ideology,* he concluded that the United States was reaching unprecedented levels of wealth inequality and that

> inequality varies widely in time and space, in structure as well as magnitude. Changes have occurred rapidly in ways that contemporaries could not have imagined only a short while before they came about. Misfortune did sometimes follow. Broadly speaking, however,

political processes, including revolutionary
transformations, that led to a reduction of
inequality proved to be immensely successful.
From them came our most precious
institutions—those that have made human
progress a reality, including universal suffrage,
free and compulsory schools, universal health
insurance, and progressive taxation. In all
likelihood the future will be no different.
The inequalities and institutions that exist
today are not the only ones possible, whatever
conservatives may say to the contrary. Change
is permanent and inevitable.

The data on which Piketty based his arguments
went back hundreds of years. It was published online,
and cited by elements of both left and right.

As the one percent pursued its professional life,
arguments like Piketty's permeated every field. "Share-
holder Value Is No Longer Everything, Top CEOs
Say," ran a 2019 *New York Times* headline. By virtue of
their educations, one percenters were not only aware
of these ideas but armed to avoid the epistemological
traps—social media algorithms, "filter bubbles"—that
prevented so many from taking them seriously. Indeed,
they appreciated the data and often agreed with the
analysis—save a single, key point: *In all likelihood the
future will be no different.*

Atop The Fortress walls, such people believed that

no matter how many elites had been replaced or over-thrown when inequality became sufficiently extreme, the historical pattern wouldn't repeat. Those who took the pattern seriously tended to believe that if it did repeat, it would do so only after they were dead. Or at least after the next election or three, at which time they would move to Norway, New Zealand, Costa Rica, et cetera. Thus they judged business as usual, but with an escape hatch, to be the wisest course of action.

Perhaps this was to be expected. Judgment, like writing, comes of one's own experience, and the experience of elites left and right in their professional lives was of unshakable security. This was true even for elites who traveled far afield, among people who might not confirm—might even criticize—their judgment. It was true for elites whose own families were cloven by political disagreement, sons and daughters left of fathers being the classic example. Even the disowned were rich. One percenters might lose in a day of trading, get laid off in the recession, might even have to sell the yacht—"we never sailed it anyway"—but they could still go out to dinner most nights. There would be no transformation that revoked the essential privileges of their lives: exclusive education and health care, multiple homes, insulation from state violence. Such a transformation might result in a better, more humane society, or simply in a new one, equally flawed but in different ways. In either case, the one percent was not interested.

Piketty, however, was not calling for such a transformation. His work emerged in the context of gradual movement by the center left, in recent decades, from welfare capitalism toward socialism and wealth redistribution. And his proposals—like a 90 percent tax on wealth over $1 billion to fund a universal inheritance, at age twenty-five, of $132,000—would allow *most* of the one percent to maintain its habits: "Under Piketty's preferred system of taxation," reported *The New Yorker,* "it would be exceedingly difficult to maintain fortunes greater than thirty-eight million dollars or so." The proposals focused instead on redistribution from a sliver of society at the very top of the one percent. Capital structures could be reformed rather than destroyed. Still, most elites, by action and inaction, opposed such proposals. Secure in their careers, comfortable with the status quo, they focused not on the public sphere but on their private lives. And in this arena, in my experience, the one percent was not quite so disproportionately successful.

The one percent, as I knew it, was sexually precocious. I remember discussion among my peers of blow jobs in the high hedges of the Hamptons when we were not yet teenagers. Courtship could become quite exotic, and also sometimes frightening. The predators, after all, had enormous resources. A young scholar once told me how, at a prestigious gallery opening in

Moscow, she'd been asked out by a prominent donor to her university. He was decades older, and she politely turned him down, thinking little of it. She lived in England at the time and, landing at Heathrow on the way home, was surprised to find a chauffeur with a sign bearing her name. She hadn't been expecting anyone. The chauffeur told her that he had been sent by the donor to take her to Claridge's, or some other five-star hotel, where he was waiting. The young scholar declined the unsettling proposal and turned to walk away—but the chauffeur chased after, pleading that she come with him. He intimated that his job, perhaps his safety, were at risk if he failed in his task. She declined again, unnerved, and escaped. There were far more horror stories, in the style of Epstein and Weinstein, than were ever known.

There was also joy. Some one percenters suspected, and had read, that joy wasn't contingent on luxury—but then, if they had the money, why not spend it? And so courtships were extravagant in the style of *Crazy Rich Asians* or James Bond or *Gossip Girl* or whatever fantasy the players preferred, made real by cash. Candlelit yoga in Ubud, Bali; sport fishing on Bristol Bay, Alaska; eating out of a silver dog bowl in Berlin's KitKatClub at the direction of a dominatrix; sex in a tuxedo in London's locked Cadogan Gardens. Or just packed with the friend group around a marble bar in the West Village, drinking a few twenty-dollar cocktails, laughing about whatever was trending on Netflix.

Subsequent weddings were extravagant. I was a groomsman at a particularly elaborate one, between old friends of mine, at a private club in Manhattan. Actually, two clubs. The ceremony and afternoon reception were conducted in a coed arts club, the Century, and the evening reception at a men's club, The Brook. These clubs, decorated much like Harvard's final clubs, counted among their members some of the most powerful people in the United States, from across the establishment political spectrum. But they were a throwback, and most weddings in the upper class occurred on city rooftops or at country houses, estates, or hotels. The sensual pleasures were wonderful: the grain of starched white tablecloths, the chilled Sancerre, the massive arrangements of calla lilies. Because the event was unique and not, one hoped, to be repeated, more money than usual was justified—for who would begrudge the bride more lilies on her wedding day, or the groom his favorite band flown in from their college town to play the reception? Not, as a rule, great dancers, the one percent. But we had enthusiasm—a great deal of which was necessary to sustain guests over the course of these multiday celebrations and the bachelor/ette parties that preceded them. I attended as many as I could and frequently gave toasts, though I never officiated.

I might well have. My particular slice of the elite was mostly agnostic or atheist, and the officiant was often a friend of the bride and groom, ordained online

and thus legally equipped, in certain states, to per-
form the marriage. The one percent's religious traditions were in decline, but syncretic new ones were on
the rise. Ceremonies were moving, even approached
the sacred, as promises made in public sometimes do.
Supernaturalism, however, was rare. Instead, the ceremonies and receptions reinforced love for one another,
for community, and, without saying so, for the concentration of power. Nothing about the weddings gave
this away, really, but one detail: One percenters wed
almost exclusively within their class.

This was the case, to take another example, at the
wedding of a college classmate in Spain. It seemed to
be attended entirely by financiers celebrating the marriage of a Norwegian and a Brit who'd met, as their
wedding website noted, at an embassy event in Jakarta.
The wedding was being held in Barcelona because the
bride's parents had a vacation home nearby, I heard, but
I didn't know the details. I was at the extreme periph-
ery of events, had gone to college with the groom but
barely knew him, and was surprised I'd been invited at
all. He ran a venture capital firm investing mostly in
software. The welcome reception was held on the terrace of a W Hotel. Waitstaff served canapés and glasses
of Alvarinho. An architect talked about how much he
loved living in Hong Kong. An ER physician, the sole
Black woman in attendance, explained how to drain
blood from a smashed fingernail. An investor with
whom I'd taken a world prehistory class detailed his

PR trials following the dissolution of a start-up, then noted casually that he'd won several seven-figure settlements in the dispute.

The next afternoon, some two hundred of us, sweating in tuxedos and ball gowns, boarded charter buses to an eleventh-century castle outside the city. Enormous cypress trees lined the grounds. White folding chairs, a parasol on each, shone in the late-afternoon sun. Four bars—two standard, one for champagne and cucumber water, one for Campari and Aperol—anchored the vast lawn. The Campari bar, oddly, doubled as a piano. A string quartet played over the burble of a tall stone fountain. Everyone was hot and eager for the ceremony to begin.

When, finally seated, all opened their parasols for shade, only a minority of us could see the bride, groom, or officiant—who, I heard, came with the castle. He was well amplified and recited in a plummy British accent the wedding website copy. He mentioned the bride and groom's various employers—among them Hilton and McKinsey—as well as Harvard and the Norwegian special forces, in which the groom and both of his brothers had served. When the officiant was finished, he invited the bride and groom to exchange vows, which they did unamplified, purposefully keeping what they said to themselves. Everyone seemed eager for a drink by the end of the ceremony and dispersed rapidly to the lawn, where a piano player soon sat down at the Campari bar keyboard. One of the waitresses set up a snare drum beside him and a third began to sing jazz standards. After drinks, we walked up the stone steps to the castle, where long tables had been set. The men joked about taking off their tuxedo jackets, then didn't for a long time. Chandeliers had been strung from the trees.

Talk at dinner was again of business, though I could not always tell what businesses were being talked about. I sat beside a Greek-Italian who invested in pharmaceuticals—remarketing generics at a markup, he explained. The master of ceremonies joked about the international nature of the proceedings: *Thank you for flying in from Singapore, Italy, Australia, the States, Norway, London . . . and Bulgaria? Do we have* Bulgaria *here?*

At brunch on a seaside terrace the next afternoon, nursing a mild hangover, I chatted with a ship broker. As we ate paella, he explained the intricacies of the container ship business. The global fleet was sixty to seventy thousand ships, and some five hundred brokers did all the deals among an ever-smaller number of owners. He explained that the most ruthless, daring ship owners managed to do business even in times of war—running blockades to Yemen, or Crimea, or Kuwait—when their insurers balked. He himself owned a stake in some ships, as well as a variety of other assets. He played the market, he told me. On the day Russia invaded Ukraine, for example, he bought a great deal of stock in Lockheed Martin, the weapons manufacturer. He knew, he said, that war would be good for business.

"If it wasn't me," he said, "someone else would have done it."

At that point, our conversation was cut short by the arrival of the investor I knew from prehistory who had won the seven-figure settlements. Soon the ship broker had to leave, to pick up his children and continue his holiday.

After the weddings, one percenter babies arrived, unsurprisingly, in equally rarefied settings. Some of the world's finest hospitals were in Manhattan and provided a range of options, from the single room a magazine editor like my father could afford back in the 1980s all the way up to birthing suites in the style of four-star hotels, occupied by moguls and movie stars. Still, some wealthy people preferred to give birth at home. Senior physicians had often known one or both of the parents, or grandparents, for decades. Some of these physicians—and dentists, therapists, and so on— kept their offices in thickly carpeted mansions off Fifth Avenue and maintained on-site X-ray and MRI devices for immediate use by their patients. Such physicians were free with their personal phone numbers and for some patients made house calls and pharmacological and surgical exceptions. One, who treated my own parents, had as an eccentric favor once jarred and given me a bit of scar tissue cut from my chin. One percenters gravitated to physicians who not only practiced but were themselves successful entrepreneurs in medical technology or pharmaceuticals, and so had at their disposal powerful networks in addition to their expertise.

Whether on account of or despite this maximal attention and care, it was a point of pride among some to give birth without the aid of anesthetics, in as "natural" a manner as possible—even if they were taking, for example, antianxiety medication. Everything we do is, of course, "natural" in the evolutionary sense. What is at issue is preference. Medical care of a certain caliber was totally preference driven. The offices of the best "concierge" physicians could make arrangements to deliver a baby internationally, if so desired. It was perhaps reassuring to know that their child could be safely born wherever convenient. Especially in the summer months, if a child was born at a hospital in New York City, the parents might be eager to take him or her immediately to a country house in Connecticut, Wyoming, Maine, or the like. Whether they stayed in the city or went to the country, a nursery would have been prepared and stocked, and, crucially, a nanny would be waiting.

Nannies were integral, ubiquitous, and carefully screened. Over a dozen candidates might be interviewed, and entire agencies existed to facilitate the process. Nannies might come from the Americas, Ireland, the Philippines—really anywhere, except their bosses' neighborhoods. The people I knew liked to see their nannies prosper. A media executive once recalled to me how one morning he was drinking coffee in his kitchen when his Polish housekeeper, who was ironing his trousers beside him, got a phone call. She took it and began yelling over the line. When she hung up, he asked, "Who was that you were speaking to?" She replied, "My Albanian housekeeper!" He loved the story. But nannies, of course, did not usually have nannies, even if they were well compensated, their children's educations were paid for, and their bosses treated them by and large with respect. After all, they lived together.

Elite children tended to love their nannies, as children cannot help but love their caregivers. This love was consequential for the ruling class. Its children sometimes felt as close to their nannies as to their own parents, or even closer. From birth, one of their most intimate relationships was transactional. The parents sometimes felt uneasy about this but believed they had no time for childcare, having to keep their prestigious jobs, and besides, they knew no other way. They were often still in touch with their own nannies, though not so much as they claimed. Only two nannies, in my experience, were invited to the weddings of the children for whom they had cared.

Who were mine? I'll leave out their names. Two were Irish, two Bolivian; one, an outlier, was male, white, from Nevada, in his early twenties. My father helped him get a job in publishing. He quit and we never heard from him again, though I tried to contact him a few times. Another, a woman, drove the family Suburban with such abandon that I went flying across the vehicle and smacked into the window. It seemed like a game. I liked it, asked her to do it more, she did. I have vivid memories of her and others, but have forgotten some too. I am in touch with only one.

I was closest to Adella. Adella lived in Jersey City, a ninety-minute train ride from the Upper East Side apartment where she cooked me dinner, bathed me, and threatened to box my ears. As a child, I liked to imitate her accent, though I did not know where it came from: Saint Vincent, a Caribbean island in the Lesser Antilles. The island was violently colonized and renamed by Europeans, though not, as sometimes asserted, by Christopher Columbus in his *Niña, Pinta,* and *Santa Maria* on January 22, 1498. According to his own papers, Columbus didn't depart Spain for the Americas until May of that year. In any case, Saint Vincent had been inhabited for millennia prior by indigenous people, who called it Hairouna, and in 2001 the nation's parliament abolished January 22's "Discovery Day" in favor of March 14's "National Heroes' Day."

Adella and I never talked about any of this, or about any of the relevant monopolies on violence that were, partly, the reason she worked for my parents rather than the reverse. We talked instead about the quotidian: *MacGyver*—which we both liked, though I suspect for different reasons; what was for dinner—carrots and I better eat them; how stubborn my brother could be—

"That big-headed boy, I'll box his ears." Being a child, I took her simply as she seemed to me: wry, consistent, beautiful, and on speaking terms with the Lord regarding my bad behavior and the patience thereby required of her. She left us when I was about twelve years old and for a long time after I was not in touch with her. I loved Adella unquestioningly, but, as I got older, communicated only as was convenient.

I'm not proud of this. We stay in touch more these days, by text and the occasional call. (When I told her about this book, she observed, "Some rich people are really nice, and some are really, really crappy.") She often invites me to her house; I've only been once. It's on a block lined with modest midcentury brick and frame houses like hers, and one year, for a late Christmas gift, I delivered an expensive cardigan.

"Boy, what have you done!? You shouldn't have done this!"

Adella scowled. She wasn't just being polite about the cardigan. I got the sense that she would have preferred the cash I spent on it, and why not? Post-nannying, she got a bachelor's degree in business administration and a job, off her feet, at TIAA-CREF, a massive financial services company. But she's had periods of joblessness, been late on her mortgage and afraid of losing her house. She'd moved to the United States, originally, to escape an abusive husband.

At the coffee table in her cluttered living room, beneath framed photographs of her family, me, my brother, and the couple other white kids she once cared for, she watched me eat reheated lasagna and asked when I planned to have children—not soon enough, in her opinion. I drank pineapple juice as we traded news. She'd recently been scammed on Facebook and was, she told me, depressed. Her son had been threatened by some toughs on Saint Vincent. In another branch of the family, a fight was under way for her dead husband's house. Before I left, she insisted on giving me some crystalware. She says I am always welcome, and that she never hears from the other children she took care of.

I tell myself I should visit more often. And I could, at this moment, make my way to Jersey City, sit on her sofa, celebrate the *MacGyver* reboot. Always, though, something rises up in me against the trip. I am too busy. But too busy with what? Part of it, simply, is life moving along. But I know also that my busyness, such as it is, speaks to a selectively forgetful—she cleaned out my ears!—narcissism, compounded by conditioning to look always toward a sparkling future rather than an unjust past and present. Visiting Adella in Jersey takes me out of The Fortress.

A place, I insist to myself, I am trying to leave. After all, if I went by Uber, I might get picked up by Michael from that hospital morgue in Brooklyn, and we got along fine. Indeed, on one of the few shifts we worked together, I was proud when he talked shit about white people but included me in the conversation—"no dis-respect." This pride echoed a handful of friendships and some reporting I'd done when subjects, Afghans and Iraqis, criticized Americans in my presence, e.g., screaming over a corpse—"America, America, America, they kill more than they liberate!"—letting me into a private part of their lives despite the violence American elites had done to them. Surely, I think sometimes, I have left The Fortress.

And yet. I've been to Europe and Asia and Africa many times but only twice to the South Bronx. I preferred to visit Iraq and Afghanistan than Mott Haven or Morrisania, or even Harlem, blocks from where I grew up. In this I was like most of the elite. The Fortress has no geography, it's inside my head. And that "pride" I felt: how few times I've felt it; how novel it remains; how shallow that it registers as pride at all; that, indeed, it's a feeling I am always trying to "get"— except perhaps when I'm too tired, too content, too occupied with my own family. And the drawbridge rises again.

III

In June 2020, the president of the Ford Foundation, Darren Walker, contributed an op-ed to *The New York Times* headlined "Are You Willing to Give Up Your Privilege?" He wrote:

> Here are a few of the special privileges and
> benefits we should be willing to surrender:
> the intricate web of tax policies that bolster
> our wealth; the entrenched system in
> American colleges of legacy admissions,
> which gives a leg up to our children; and
> above all, the expectation that, because of our
> money, we are entitled to a place at the front
> of the line.

As I read, I knew the ruling class would never surrender these privileges. Some would refuse purely out of greed. Most would refuse for lack of imagination and experience. Mr. Walker clearly had both. As noted in his piece, he grew up in the bottom one percent and ascended to the top. He had seen excellence and possibility at many socioeconomic levels. But the ruling class did not have this breadth. It did not know, and so could not believe, that anything less expensive and exclusive than its own schools or clubs or hospitals or political parties could really be as good. To accept as much called into question the concentration of resources and effort that such institutions required, and so the history, and very identities, of the families involved. Were the privileges that Mr. Walker mentioned ever surrendered, private schools like Buckley, for example, might struggle to exist. Whatever the values engraved on silver cups awarded ninth graders, the school depended on three simple ideas: The best education—"front of the line"—was worth a great deal of money; legacies built a strong community that kept the money flowing; and gifts to the school were a collective good, appropriately incentivized in the tax code. How otherwise, members of the board might ask, are we to maintain the capital campaign? To attract talent like Fogarty? To run annual trips to Washington to meet senators? To keep enrollment down? To do away with tax deductions and legacies would be to deny board members' children what their parents had enjoyed. To reform the institution so radically would be to dismantle it, thus betraying the traditions—the teachers!—that defined the childhoods of its graduates. It would change fundamental values. And one percenters rarely made fundamental changes—even when, eventually, they realized their own mortality.

———

For some, that moment arrived with the draw of a wild card: serious illness, a suicide, a freak accident. I went to school with a boy, for example, who fell off a billiards table in his family "barn" in the Hamptons onto a pool cue, which skewered him and then snapped. His mildly intoxicated adolescent peers rushed across the street to the main house to alert his father, who helped him into a truck and onward to the hospital. He survived, but only by a lucky break.

More often, intimations of mortality arrived as one percenters ushered parents through death, however well staffed the transition might be. And what then, as death came into view? Days passed more quickly, seasons blurred. Many, in response, tried to "optimize" their lives—and not just the technologists. No elite could escape the behavioral data extraction and modification, phone by bed, for example, that surveillance capitalism entailed, even if they were its main beneficiaries. Likewise, none could avoid the changing climate their industrial empires wrought. They exploited not only the ninety-nine percent but themselves and their own world.

Along the way, in search of meaning, they threw themselves into the rhythms of wealth, a carousel of school plays, quarterly bonuses, summering and wintering, philanthropy. Plenty of time for reflection on the chair lift. Lives were scheduled years into the future. One knew, for example, with whom and where one would be lunching the day after next year's gala for the Central Park Conservancy or the Koch Theater. Such one percenters aspired to a "frictionless" existence, which money made, superficially, possible. It was easy to love such people at their lavish but tasteful holiday parties, caroling as black-clad caterers refilled champagne flutes.

The inevitable middle-age crises were extravagant. One black-tie wedding reception sticks in memory for the SWAT team that arrived in response to a bomb threat called in by the groom's ex-wife—to my knowledge, she wasn't charged. I was a child at the time, dressed in a linen suit, cooed over by women who, over the years, appeared to become addicted to cosmetic surgery. Drug problems were also common. Asking for news of people I went to school with, I've heard more than once, "He's either rich or dead." People who had been encouraged to take Ritalin or Adderall since childhood to ensure academic success found themselves depending on drugs at the bank, on the slopes, at home—until they collapsed. These are perennially popular stories in part because the falls were hard. Consider a once handsome hedge funder brought low and bloated, alienated from his children, ousted from his job, weeping into his vodka beside silver-framed photos of his youth. Such suffering was often proportionate to the confidence lost, and the self-loathing was immense. One of The Fortress's great cruelties, for its inhabitants, was the illusion that it could keep out pain.

So the walls were built ever higher. In old age, one percenters venerated each other, saw even less of the outside world. They lived longer than the ninety-nine and in greater health. From the bottom step of the Metropolitan Museum of Art, following Buckley's hundredth-anniversary gala—the one held in the shadow of the Temple of Dendur—I watched a renowned artist and fellow alumnus, at that time in his eighties, slide down the banister in a black velvet smoking jacket. Landing beside me, he bummed a cigarette, then disappeared into a waiting car with a woman my own age, perhaps his daughter, though likely, it seemed to me, not. Others, with less panache, were no less vigorous. Some even investigated the haunted science of life extension. Google's Calico (standing for California Life Company) is reported, somewhat sensationally, to be trying to "solve death." Its efforts to combat aging are in scale less dramatic, but the talent and ambition—some would say hubris—required are still awe-inspiring. "We are not a traditional biotechnology company," runs the company website, "nor are we an academic institution. We look to combine the best parts of both without the constraints of either."

I wonder how we'll fare if the richest among us do regularly begin living into their hundreds. Some of the oldest are already causing the biggest problems. The average senator is aged sixty-four and can expect to exert his influence long after leaving office. The presidential candidates in 2020 were seventy-four and seventy-seven, respectively. That the pursuit of power at such age might itself suggest a lack of wisdom is not a widely considered possibility. That it be handed over to anyone outside The Fortress, almost unthinkable.

Also, given the status quo, unlikely. One percenters dominate global leadership. With few exceptions, we remain governed by the rich. They trade presidencies, Congresses, courts, et cetera, back and forth. What peaceful transitions of power transpire are no small feat. But it is difficult to ignore the fact that our leaders are mostly one percenters. The rich do not give up power.

Not even, if they can help it, in death. The dead derive their power from memory—and elites do all they can to ensure sure their dead are remembered. "The job of peasants is to stay out of the archives," observed the scholar James C. Scott. Rich people, on the other hand, take up historical space. Which is why I can describe, based on sources from the time, the funeral of B. Lord Buckley. It wasn't so different from some I've attended myself.

On December 28, 1932, more than seven hundred mourners mounted the steps of Saint Thomas Church in midtown Manhattan. They walked through its massive doors, beneath statues of martyrs, scholars, warriors, and the patron saint of skeptics himself, Thomas. The day was cold. Inside, winter light filtered through some ten thousand panes of stained glass onto a crowd dense with alumni of Buckley's school. His close friend President-Elect Franklin Delano Roosevelt, though absent, was listed on the program as an honorary pall-bearer. FDR's sons Franklin Jr. and John found their seats among their classmates in the dark pews. The reverend rector and his assistant—a Columbia University classmate of Buckley's—began with a reading from scripture, then led the assembled in song. *Lead thou me on!*

The hush after the hymn was followed by the Apostles' Creed, the Lord's Prayer, and a final blessing from the reverend. He carried a bouquet of lilies from the altar to the coffin, which was blanketed in lavender sweet peas and yellow roses. A Supreme Court justice, a future ambassador, a journalist, and a couple of financiers bore the coffin out to Fifth Avenue and eventually Woodlawn Cemetery. In furs, fedoras, and overcoats, mourners dispersed into the fourth winter of the Great Depression.

Around the city, families waited in line for bread.

We are all products of a class. But what sets a person askew of that class? There is a long tradition of elites who question their position and pursue reform—like FDR—or even revolution. Mikhail Bakunin, for example, an early anarchist, was born to an aristocratic family but wrote, in *God and the State,* "It is the characteristic of privilege and every privileged position to kill the mind and heart of men."

This seems to me an extreme opinion, but I can

imagine how a person appalled by hypocrisy might come to it. Off the page, Bakunin socialized with and criticized elites who grappled with their privilege. One was Friedrich Engels, who famously used a family fortune derived from Manchester textile factories to support his writing partner, Karl Marx. Marx, for his part, was not wealthy and rarely had enough money to live in his preferred style—rejuvenating on the Isle of Wight, for example. But criticizing capitalism didn't stop him from enjoying its luxuries or mourning their absence. He is remembered to have said of his magnum opus, "*Capital* will not pay for the cigars I smoked writing it."

Such thinkers inform today's elite critics of the one percent, often in ways we don't, or can't, fully articulate. But understanding a person's intellectual genealogy is only one way of explaining their political beliefs. Another way—and more interesting to most people, in my experience—is personal history. The philosopher John Gray takes this method to an extreme, channeling the founder of psychoanalysis. "Freud taught," he writes, "that for any human being, kindness or cruelty, having a sense of justice or lacking it, depends on accidents of childhood. We all know this to be true, but it goes against much of what we say we believe. We cannot give up the pretense that being good is something anyone can achieve."

I hope, to the contrary, that a sense of justice depends more on free will than accidents of childhood.

But I recognize also that my own attitudes were largely inherited from, and developed in reaction to, my parents. My mother was the daughter of Lithuanian and Polish immigrants to Springfield, Massachusetts. Nazis killed several of her aunts and maternal grandparents. A family of entrepreneurial scrap metal traders, the survivors prospered in the United States and sent her to private school. My father was raised by a single public school teacher from a farm in Solon Springs, Wisconsin, that lacked indoor plumbing. He became a prominent magazine editor, writer, and media executive; my mother a book editor and novelist. Both knew how rare my childhood was, how strange to fly on a private jet, even if it belonged to my father's boss.

When I aged out of the Junior Yacht program, they helped me get a job. I worked that summer at a restaurant called Maya's, which sat on the south side of Route 27 in Wainscott, New York. A *New York Times* review, headlined "A Hot Import from St. Barts," observed that its "dishes are speedily whisked from the kitchen, but the young men doing the whisking haven't a clue as to who ordered them." I was one of the clueless young men. Several of us teenage busboys were children of the proprietress's social circle. One, I remember, asked me why I cared so much as he watched me furiously slicing bread. I shrugged and kept slicing while he snuck out to get high. I was that sort of kid: intense, ambitious, rule-abiding. The waitresses were often frustrated with me. I once spilled a decorative bowl of apples across the table where Billy Joel was dining with his daughter. I took it on myself to pour wine, then poured incorrectly, garnering complaints. I was a clumsy busboy.

The next June, I asked my parents if, instead of working at Maya's, I could write a novel. They encouraged me to try, and I wrote a coming-of-age novel that both critiqued the Upper East Side elite and exemplified its insularity. In September, when I finished the manuscript, my parents read it, liked it, and sent it to a close friend who owned a publishing house. I remember asking my father repeatedly if he thought his friend would publish it. "He might" was the answer. I fervently hoped so. The publisher soon invited me to his paper-strewn office off Union Square, where he offered me twenty-five thousand dollars to publish the book. Thereafter, my experience became even more unusual, as the book sold several hundred thousand copies, received good reviews, and was published in more than twenty languages. I was flown to Australia and half a dozen European countries to give readings. Someone bought the movie rights, and soon I sold another novel. I was a rich person, getting richer—as a writer, no less.

I was glad my parents hadn't told me to go back to work as a busboy. Occasionally I allowed myself to believe that my success had as much to do with hard work as the circumstances into which I was born. But most of the press and reviews, I found, raised questions of elitism and nepotism. I became, in a small way, a symbol of privilege. And this, it turned out, set me even *more* askew of my class than my parents had. I began to realize, from reading the critics, talking with peers, and eventually reporting on violence and deprivation, that while my work was sufficient, my circumstances were necessary to whatever modest success I achieved. I began to see how, in the United States of America and elsewhere, success almost always, and predominantly, depends upon wealth—and frequently comes at the expense of the less wealthy. My book was published because I had the connections to get it looked at; it took attention from novelists who were not as rich or white or connected as me.

This was sometimes difficult to accept. We in the one percent like to believe in meritocracy, even fairness. These ideas are beloved by media and one of the few bipartisan talking points. Barack Obama: "Anything is possible in America." Donald Trump: "In America, anything is possible." Famous examples demonstrate the seductive drama of economic mobility but obscure its frequency. Henry Ford was the son of a farmer. A century later, Darren Walker was born to a nurse's aide. Steve Jobs, Oprah Winfrey, George Soros—and so on in every profession. Such examples not only make one percenters feel good, they distract from the possibility of a more humane distribution of wealth.

One percenters who pursue that possibility are often born outside The Fortress, but sometimes they aren't. Both types try to knock down its walls on a personal scale, and are often worldly, compassionate, and measured. Again thanks to my parents, I got to know an old man like that—Peter Matthiessen—in Tanzania, after I finished college. They were friends with him, and that summer he was leading a bird-watching trip to raise money for a Buddhist charity—the Zen Peacemakers—and invited me along, free of charge. Peter was a writer, mostly, and cofounder of a famous literary magazine in Paris in the 1950s. Since then he'd joined a variety of campaigns in alliance with indigenous peoples. He'd also done much acid and studied in Japan to become a Zen *roshi*. All this was made possible, initially, by the wealth into which he'd been born. But by the end of his life that fortune seemed to be gone, and he lived relatively simply. Though his work still carried him around the world, many years earlier he had turned against elite systems of power. One afternoon on the Tanzanian savanna, looking for a rare bird of some kind or another—an emerald-spotted dove, I believe—he confided that he didn't have many regrets in life, that really only one came to mind: being a spy. The magazine in the 1950s, it turned out, had been a front for the CIA. Peter had been spying on communists.

"I realized I liked the people I was spying on better than the people I was spying for," he told me.

At home in Long Island, Peter lived close to the ocean. On a different afternoon, years later, we walked from his house to the beach. He wanted to go swimming but warned me that he was not strong enough to keep his feet in the waves, and so I might have to help him. He entered the water elegantly but, as predicted, did not have the strength to get out on his own; the shore break, small as it was, batted him about until I put an arm around his waist, then another beneath his knees, and carried him up onto the fine sand. It was a warm and windy day. He was, at that point, already suffering the cancer that would kill him. I remember how achingly slender he was, his bones, the tendons behind his knee, which pressed against my forearm, his loose skin, spotted with age and wet with seawater. Once we were settled he rested on his flank, supporting his head in a hand, completely (so it seemed to me) unself-conscious about his weakness, how he'd fallen in the waves, our momentary physical intimacy. When he died not long after, he left me the collected works of the comic novelist P. G. Wodehouse, whose greatest creations—Wooster and Jeeves—are a clueless aristocrat and brilliant valet. I suspect in this he was telling me to lighten up. Like some few one percenters I've known, he seemed totally unafraid.

I suppose forty years of Zen training helps with that. But there were surely easier ways for rich people to learn their fears were not, in fact, so fearful. That wealth made life easier, but that joy was available without hierarchy, and that insulation from the world's harshest pains—hunger, infant mortality, cruel illiteracy—was not, really, so expensive. Didn't have to be, anyway, if the elite shared power more widely.

In any case, no matter how rich, no matter how

long they live, one percenters, like everyone else, have a finite time in which to think on these problems. I have now and then encountered the dead and dying— "One, two, three," Jawann would say in the morgue, and we'd hoist a body—and even, on a handful of occasions, thought I myself might die quite a bit sooner than I'd like. My mind went, in several of those moments, to people I have loved. I'm not certain that proximity to death provides any greater clarity, but I know that a final movement of the mind to love is common and has nothing to do with wealth or power. Asking elites to consider their mortality is not a winning strategy for more equitable society, I suppose, but the question lies beneath everything else. In the back of Buckley's newsletter, which arrives in my mailbox, on heavy stock, several times a year, is a section titled *in memoriam:* '39, '44, '52, '53, '54, '67, '96, run the numbers, ever higher.

I V

There were only sixteen of us in my ninth-grade class, so it was not difficult to contact them all. I wanted to know what they thought about our education and lives to date as a starting point for conversations about wealth, race, and power.

Of the fifteen besides myself, nine responded to my email, and eight agreed to be recorded: an investment banker, a research analyst at an asset management firm, two partners at private equity firms, two journalists, a media executive, and a corporate lawyer. Six were white, one was mixed race, Chinese-Caucasian. The eighth, whom I'd always considered white, said it was more complicated than that and revealed that he had a Latinx parent. This was not the only surprise. Though I had not seen or spoken with most of these classmates for more than two decades, our conversations were intimate and wide-ranging. We were nearly forty.

What follows are excerpts of what they said. Though some agreed to speak on the record, others preferred to remain anonymous, and I have left out all their identities. None of them claimed or wished to speak for the one percent, but each was a product of it.

We talked on a walk around Brooklyn, high in a midtown office tower, around my kitchen table, over lunch at a restaurant on the Bowery, or by Zoom.

Mostly we told stories, as I have in the preceding pages. This is best done with an awareness not only of perspective but of the many other ways of understanding. The neuroendocrinologist and primatologist Robert Sapolsky, in his book *Behave,* walks the reader backward through time and across disciplines. "A behavior has just occurred," he writes. "Why did it happen?" He charts a path through neurobiology; then the sensory stimuli that trigger our nervous systems; then the hormones that determine how responsive we are to those stimuli. Then childhood, fetal environment, genetic makeup. "And then," he writes, "you increase the view to encompass factors larger than that one individual—how has culture shaped the behavior of people living in that individual's group?—what ecological factors helped shape that culture—expanding and expanding until considering events umpteen millennia ago and the evolution of that behavior."

I can't really keep all that in mind when I think about the one percent, my classmates, or anyone else in these pages. But I do remember, usually, that there's no simple explanation for why people act the way they do. We don't even know ourselves, much of the time. And what we see in ourselves, when we really look, can be unsettling. There's a part of me, for example, that wants to be even richer (much richer!) than I am now—and anyway what's so wrong with that?! But other voices quiet that one. There's a particularly strong one now, here in my head, insisting: *All this is obvious, childish, soft, naïve! Take a stand! Admit no uncertainty! Confidence wins the day!*

In speaking to my old classmates, I tried to understand how they grappled with their own clashing voices. I also aimed to improve the accuracy of my recollections and reporting. While I did not fact-check everything they said, I got the sense that these classmates of mine were telling the truth, best they could. The only exception was one who told me he voted for Trump in 2016, but not in 2020. "We let the genie out of the bottle," he said, and claimed not to support any election-denying candidates, anymore. When I googled him, though, I found that he did. He had been perhaps the most vocally political of us at Buckley, and that's more or less where I began the interviews.

How, I asked them all, *did you end up there?*

"Well, my grandfather had gone there. My dad went there. So that was it. As far as my dad was concerned, I was gonna go there, end of story."

"My family was newly wealthy, and not even that wealthy by New York standards. I didn't have generational experience on the Upper East Side . . . not that we didn't have some money. But I hadn't been exposed to that kind of wealth, or just sort of the WASPy culture of the place. And I see that as, like, a good thing and a bad thing. Like, I'm glad I was exposed to it, because I understand it now, and can, I think, in large part because of my time at Buckley, know how to navigate it."

"We had a far more economically diverse class than both of my brothers had. . . . My younger brother is great. He has a heart of gold. But I joke that he, like, collects billionaires as a hobby."

"It's all ancient history but, you know, my dad grew up in a house designed by Stanford White."

"Yeah, there's another view of it as being this machine that's producing certain types of people. But then again, when I do any sort of analysis, it's like, no, these are all just—almost everybody in our class, at least—just kind of normal dudes, with normal families, and some people have cool jobs. Again, I don't think of our class as being like a microcosm necessarily of the Buckley experience. . . . But maybe I'm wrong."

———

"What you're saying is that how the one percent is created is actually perpetuating power dynamics—it's a machine instead of a museum. I think—I'm just totally BS-ing right now—that's probably true for half the class. The other half of the class is like, truly, they're fuckups."

"You train them as leaders. Even at a very, very young age, and they go on to other institutions that foster those leadership qualities, and they have enough ambition. You're gonna see a lot of people that are in positions of power, politically, in business, forever. And then you have to look at them as people. Okay, so you're the governor, the director of the FBI, the head of Morgan Stanley, you're head of whatever. Are you doing the right thing?"

"I don't know, I think it's hard for me to assess whether I would put myself in that category of being produced by a machine. I'd like to think that . . . not."

"Going back to [our headmaster] . . . I feel like he had some sort of an uncanny ability to pick young boys who would turn into very large young men. I don't know how he did it. . . . And as a result, our football team, our wrestling team, just trounced other teams in sports. It was humiliating for other schools in a kind of bizarre way. And it was a point of pride for Buckley boys, right, like the 120 consecutive meets that Buckley won in wrestling, right? Like, oh, it was a Buckley wrestling dynasty for a decade. It was outrageous."

"I was always on the smaller side of Buckley kids. And I remember at one point, everybody was kind of growing and, like, I wasn't. I was kind of falling behind the growth trajectory. I was the third or fourth smallest kid in the grade. And my mom actually took me to the doctor, and the doctor was like, 'Your son is fine. He's in the 75th percentile of height. He is *above average*.'"

"I do think that I'm a competitive person. And I think that was amplified. Or maybe even created."

"The one thing that Buckley really hammered down was—at least they tried to—they wanted to make leaders."

"There were sixteen students in the ninth-grade class, and there were, like, sixteen different extracurriculars. And [the faculty] kind of knew, by that point, who you were. The only one that actually was voted on was the school president. And so he was voted school president, and everything else was distributed like, you know, cookies."

"I'm not sure it's good for anybody to be part of something that so self-consciously is designed to produce people who run the world. You know? Because the world is changing. And, you know, the strategies for running it, they're not the same anymore. . . . I think a lot of people would have been better off with an idea that they're just . . . ordinary people."

"My girlfriend went to [an all-girls Manhattan private school] and I look at her class, and it's exactly the same as our class. They work at Google, or Goldman, or whatever."

"I'm kind of embarrassed that I say that I work in finance, right? Like I say it muttering under my breath. But when I wake up in the morning, I *like* my job. . . . I would say I've met plenty of decent people in the world of finance. But 90 percent of the people in finance are really just trying to make as much money as they humanly can. There's no love of the game."

―――――

"I don't think I [went into finance] as much because there was a clearly defined path, in the way that it may have been for some of our peers. For me, it was just like, 'Yeah, like, I want to live in New York, and I'd like to do so comfortably, and there aren't a lot of jobs that allow you to do that.'"

"I don't think I'll ever live in Manhattan again. Or really in New York City, if I'm honest . . . it's turned into this like playground of the, you know, the elite citizens of the world."

"I do think it's very hard, and potentially very destructive, to have people think that owning a ten-bedroom apartment on Park Avenue is like, sort of the norm, that's what you need to aspire to. I don't know, that's kind of sad. Because there's just so many other possibilities and outcomes. I do think we get boxed in, growing up in that environment and like, only seeing that thing. . . . Look, some people sort of break through. And like, honestly, you know, just looking at our class, I think most of the people have broken through."

"From personal experience—I hope you feel the same way—almost everybody I know from Buckley, or people who went to similar schools that we grew up with, are not cutthroat, ruthless, elitist, stuck-up people. I mean, I know very, very few people that are truly like that. And people I know that *are* like that—I think a lot of it is affected. And comes from maybe an inferiority complex. And I know that most people look down on that, especially in this day and age."

"I mean, listen, I'm not gonna send my kid to Buckley. So I'm not trying to defend Buckley. But how do you get rid of it? What do you do? There are a bunch of rich people who want to give their kids a really high-quality education. I guess my first question is, one, should they not be allowed to do that? Two, are they doing it in a horribly wrong way? And then three, if they are doing it in a horribly wrong way, how do they do it better?"

"This came up actually at the twenty-year reunion, where there were a bunch of guys who had sons, and the only person who [said he'd send his sons to Buckley] was [———]. But it's interesting, I mean, I think there are a lot of different components that went into why people thought that. I think one of the main reasons was more economic, was like, 'Why spend fifty grand to send my kids to read *Catcher in the Rye* and, like, play lacrosse, when I can go live in Bronxville and send them to the public school and have, you know, arguably, a more normal, better experience?' "

"We're sending them to a Catholic school in the neighborhood. We can afford it. It's easy to get to. And they have academic rigor, you know, trust the Jesuits for that. And they believe in teaching the kids character and manners and all that. I don't know. I mean, we still might end up sending the kids to a public school, but then things are a little more up in the air and chaotic, you know. Then you have to worry about New York City politics. You have to worry about the school boards and all that stuff. You know, you get people who are too woke for their own good, sometimes."

"Quiet street? Oh, the bus? Yeah."

"I think I must have asked like, 'Why are we being quiet here?' "

"I can't remember his name, but he was a coach . . . he told us as first graders that there was something that had happened years before, and that when we're driving down the street we can't talk. When you're six years old, things aren't as apparent and obvious to you. But I think you don't have to be that old to figure it out."

———

"You remember [another student] and how he used to sing 'Build Me Up Buttercup,' like, take his shirt off on the bus? If I was an adult having to put up with that every single day, yeah, I might make up a story about how, you know, if they didn't shut up and sit down, we would all be dragged out of the bus and necklaced like, like in South Africa or something. I can also believe that some kid did something deliberately offensive. And someone on the street threw a rock, and the bus company said, 'Hey, we're not gonna haul your dickhead children anymore unless you tell them to be quiet in this neighborhood.' As far as the actual truth of it . . . no idea."

"I remember Quiet Street very well . . . 124th? Was it 124th or 123rd? That's even *more* a reflection of New York in the '80s, in the '90s. Where you would drive through a street and it was, you know, an underprivileged area. And the bus had to be quiet because, you know, they were afraid of attracting attention to it."

"Look, the racial thing was crazy."

"I mean, hard to fill a class with racial and ethnic minorities, you know, at forty grand a year. And I can't even imagine like, what it'd be like, for the [scholar-ship] kids coming in. I mean, I haven't talked to [——]. I'd be very curious to hear his thoughts on the subject."

"One of the things my wife and I really appreciate so far about our daughter's public school is its diver-sity, about 50 percent white. Two [scholarship] kids per class isn't a reflection of the real world. You've probably already thought about this, but I'd be really interested in what [——] and other [scholarship] boys thought about their experience."

"So let me answer your question by asking *you* a question. You talked about wanting to write this book in the context of discussing issues that are broader than Buckley: race, et cetera, et cetera. Why do *you* think Buckley is relevant to that conversation?"

V

I couldn't forgive him or like him, but I saw that what he had done was, to him, entirely justified. It was all very careless and confused. They were careless people, Tom and Daisy—they smashed up things and creatures and then retreated back into their money or their vast carelessness, or whatever it was that kept them together. . . .

—F. Scott Fitzgerald, *The Great Gatsby*

In that first summer of the pandemic, after I stopped volunteering in the morgue, as food lines lengthened, the Black Lives Matter protests escalated. Tens of thousands of people filled the streets. In New York City, protestors set police cruisers ablaze and workmen nailed plywood over boutique windows in SoHo. One evening, I saw the vanguard of a crowd climb through a smashed store window on Twelfth Street, emerge with hoodies and T-shirts, and escape a handful of pudgy, outnumbered cops. A few blocks farther south, I fell in behind a gaggle of excited teenagers. "This place is done," one of them said, "let's go to Nike." In the news, such violations overshadowed far more numerous peaceful protests in New York, Minneapolis, Portland, and elsewhere, whose participants were regularly kettled, charged, and pepper-sprayed by police. None of this, in the short term, changed the balance of power or material lives of the rich or poor. But history taught that mass movements, gradually then all at once, toppled governments. Members of the ruling class knew this and were afraid.

What, exactly, did such people fear? A venture fund manager at that wedding in Barcelona told me that he expected, within his children's lifetime, widespread, violent conflict on account of resource scarcity and climate change. He was not the only one. One percenters knew the MDMA and the Veuve, the weekends in the George V, the trilingual prostitutes, the *time* to craft stories of social mobility into election campaigns, the companies valuing profit over lives, the Dubai hotels built by indentured Bangladeshis—they knew all of it cost more than what they read on their credit card statements. In their most imaginative hours, some feared the bill would come due in bloody revolution. A greater number displaced their fears onto Black teenagers, or black-clad antifascists, or American-flag-draped anti-vaxxers toting AR-15s on courthouse steps—where, in another nightmare, the bill came due before a judge.

The fear they shared was loss of wealth. Without

ever saying so, they were very much afraid of losing their country houses, the barn converted for their kids' sleepovers, the space for the grand piano, the greenhouses, the pied-à-terre where their mother-in-law stayed without being in everyone's business, the airport lounge that allowed them to enjoy pleasures among their own, in quiet. They were afraid of processed supermarket cheese, much preferred the organic stuff, which, they emphasized, would keep them alive longer. The same could not be said of their clothes, but they were afraid of losing the Prada bags anyway, the heavy zippers, the cashmere. They didn't want to wear polyester windbreakers, or sit on Ikea sofas, or drive a Hyundai. They were afraid of losing the safer, sleeker Mercedes. They were afraid of losing all of it, any of it. And who wouldn't prefer a Mercedes, anyway?

But the quality of the car was not what lay at the root of the fear. They feared losing wealth not for its own sake but because it was justified, *in their own minds,* by intelligence, hard work, determination—that is, by character. If they lost their wealth, then, well, who were they? The true fear was not loss of wealth but loss of self.

After that summer of protests, I biked uptown to Quiet Street. It was a grey morning and Manhattan's leaves were turning and beginning to fall. I made the same trip I had all those years ago, starting in front of

Buckley on Seventy-Third Street. The only people of color around were a security guard and the proprietor of a fruit stand on the corner. Up Third Avenue, traffic was mild. The city unrolled more or less uniformly until Ninety-Sixth Street, where it started to become Harlem. Twenty years of gentrification had changed some blocks but not others. The neighborhood was similar enough that I could picture it as in childhood, through the tinted windows of the charter buses.

Quiet Street, though, was not as I remembered it, lined by abandoned buildings and vacant lots. Two well-kept community gardens occupied the open spaces and none of the buildings were abandoned. That morning, with the pandemic resurgent, the block was empty. I had a hard time finding anyone to talk to. The western-most storefront was occupied by a darkened franchise of H&R Block, a Kansas–based financial services firm and frequent target, and escapee, of class action lawsuits, like one in the late aughts concerning "aggressive peddling of fee-laden retirement accounts that were virtually guaranteed to lose money," according to then New York attorney general Andrew Cuomo. In that case the company, whose 2019 revenue was $3.01 billion, agreed to settle up to $20 million, depending on the number of claims. Had every one of the more than six hundred thousand potentially wronged customers filed for restitution, each would have come away with roughly thirty-three dollars. "An H&R Block spokesman," reported Reuters, "called the New York settlement 'satisfactory for all parties.' . . . In late afternoon trading, H&R Block shares were up 7 cents." If H&R Block provided some useful services to people in Harlem, it also apparently took advantage of them, to the benefit of one percenters.

I continued down the south side of the street. Next door was an awning marked "Harlem Vet Center (Here To Serve)." After that, much of the block was taken up by a police station and its well-labeled parking spaces, e.g., "Cop Of The Month"; then two more apartment buildings, and one of the community gardens. Across the street were twelve stories of "eco-friendly luxury" rentals, the other community garden, and a parking garage. At the far end of the block, Second Avenue bustled and cars on-ramped to the Triborough Bridge, as my bus once had. On the corner, an elderly gentleman in ragged sweatpants reclined on the pavement and, as I walked by, shouted:

"Hey! I'm hungry!"

I circled the block, thinking, looking around: A List Cuts Barber Shop; Kennedy Chicken and Pizza; Chambers Memorial Baptist Church; a rising office tower; the Salvation Army's "Manhattan Citadel"; masks that read "I can't breathe"; people waiting for a bus. The city.

Back on Quiet Street, the gentleman in ragged sweatpants saw me, rose, and called out again.

"I'm hungry! Help me get some soup or something to eat!"

He mimed spooning soup. I apologized for not having any change and turned away.

On a whim, I returned to the Harlem Vet Center, though it appeared closed, and rang the bell. The door buzzed open. In a stale hallway, I was greeted by Michelle, who worked for the Department of Veterans Affairs. She was Black, middle-aged, wore a hoodie and leg brace, leaned on a cane. I introduced myself as a writer and she invited me to sit down in the common area of the office, which was, save for her and one colleague, deserted. Michelle sat straight-backed, her braced leg balanced on the cane before her. For five years she'd been in the army—an "admin soldier," she said—but had left on account of illness. We talked about the neighborhood. Above her head hung a poster of wounded American soldiers carrying each other to safety.

"It's kinda sad, what's happening since the pandemic," she told me, "the increase to homelessness is just mind-boggling."

Some of the homeless were veterans, for whom she and her colleagues provided various kinds of support. In her twelve years with the Vet Center in Harlem the situation had never been worse. The neighborhood generally was a difficult place to live, she said: "The rent is staggeringly high and you're afraid to leave your apartment." Michelle had long since moved to Yonkers with her mother and daughter. And she was frightened for that daughter, she said, on account of the coming election.

"I don't want to press on what's not my business," I said, "but why are you frightened for her?"

"I think Americans are underestimating the situation, and the reason for that is that they are not used to political violence. I'm a Jamaican. I know what political violence can do."

I agreed and we kept chatting—about the neighborhood and the election, the army and Iraq. Eventually, I told Michelle the reason I'd come to her particular block—the story of Quiet Street. How at Buckley, on our buses, we were always silent on this block, never knew why, and how later I'd heard that a white kid had yelled an epithet out the window and someone on the block had thrown something at the bus in response.

Had she ever heard about an incident like that, with a bus full of rich white kids?

Michelle told me she'd never heard about it. She shook her head, sighed, and looked away. She seemed tired and unsurprised.

For a long moment, we sat in silence. Then we carried on talking.

Acknowledgments

I am grateful for reads, edits, and good counsel on this short book from Alice Whitwham, Roopa Gogineni, Trevor Snapp, Karl Taro Greenfeld, Luke Mogelson, Samitha Mukhopadhyay, Anand Gopal, Matt Aikins, Musab Younis, James Morrissey, Casey Selwyn, Ross Perlin, Dave Evans, Aziz Isham, Ali Gharib, Eric Simonoff, Lisa Lucas, Roland Ottewell, Rita Madrigal, Amber Salik, Zach Phillips, Sara Chatta, and Joanie, Thomas, Stacey, and Terry McDonell. Any mistakes are mine alone.

A Note About the Author

Nick McDonell was born in New York City in 1984 and published his first novel, the international best seller *Twelve,* at the age of eighteen. He has since published three additional novels, five books of nonfiction on the wars in Iraq and Afghanistan, and a work of political theory on nomadism. He has contributed to *TIME, Harper's Magazine, The New Yorker, The Paris Review,* and the *London Review of Books,* and is a cofounder of the Zomia Center. McDonell graduated from Harvard University and received a master's degree in international relations from St. Antony's College, Oxford.

A Note on the Type

This book was set in a version of the well-known Monotype face Bembo. This letter was cut for the celebrated Venetian printer Aldus Manutius by Francesco Griffo, and first used in Pietro Cardinal Bembo's *De Aetna* of 1495.

The companion italic is an adaptation of the chancery script type designed by the calligrapher and printer Ludovico degli Arrighi.

Typeset by Scribe,
Philadelphia, Pennsylvania
Printed and bound by Berryville Graphics,
Berryville, Virginia
Designed by Maria Carella